CU01508630

Saragarhi: The Forgotten Battle

120th Anniversary Edition

By Jay Singh-Sohal

Third Edition published in 2017 by:

Dot Hyphen Publishers, Birmingham, UK

Copyright © Jagjeet Singh Sohal 2017

First and second edition published in 2013.

ISBN: 978-0-9570540-7-3

For Livtar

Crest of the 36th (Sikh) Regiment of Bengal Infantry.

Contents

Svaiya

Supreme Lord, grant me this boon
That I may never falter in performing righteous actions.
When I fight my enemies may I not be a bit intimidated by them,
May I be victorious.
That I may instruct my mind to continuously crave to utter Your praises.
And when my mortal life comes to an end,
May I die fighting fiercely in battle.

Sri Guru Gobind Singh ji
(Sikh national anthem)

Chronology of Events

1813:
Treaty of Gulistan signals peace between Imperial Russia and Persia, and sees the start of the classic period of the "Great Game" between Britain and Russia which runs until the Anglo-Russian Convention of 1907

1839-42:
First Anglo-Afghan War

1842:
Retreat from Kabul: more than 4,500 British and native Indian soldiers and 12,000 camp followers killed by Pathan tribesmen

1845-6:
First Anglo-Sikh War (or Sutlej campaign)

1848-9:
Second Anglo-Sikh War (or Punjab campaign) annexation of the Sikh Kingdom by the British

1849:
18th May: Disbanded Sikh units (including six infantry regiments and five cavalry) raised into the Trans-frontier Brigade by Sir Henry Lawrence and sent to Afghanistan

1851:
Trans-frontier Brigade renamed the Punjab Irregular Force (nicknamed Piffers), the first five battalions of infantry recruited from disbanded Sikh troops, the rest from across other races.

1865:
Further reorganisation of the irregulars into the Punjab Frontier Force

1878–80:
Second Anglo-Afghan War

1881:
Afridi ceasefire, Khyber Pass re-opened

1891:
Fighting on the Samana Ridge, area recovered by Sir William Lockhart. Building of forts and posts on the Samana commences

1893:
British agree borders between India and Afghanistan with the Amir

1897:
Year of Afridi and Orakzai uprising:
July: Start of the Malakand Campaign
August: Afridi attack, capture and burn forts on the Khyber line
September: Attack on the Samana, last stand at Saragarhi
October: Start of the Tirah Campaign

1898:
29th January: Death of Lt Col John Haughton, commander of the 36th Sikhs

1900:
Samana granted a battle honour and 12th September declared a regiment holiday as 'Saragarhi Day'

1901:
November: Saragarhi memorial unveiled at Fort Lockhart

1902:
16th April: Saragarhi memorial unveiled at Amritsar

1904:
18th January: Saragarhi memorial unveiled at Ferozepur

1914:
Outbreak of the Great War, ending in 1918

1919:
Third Anglo-Afghan War

Foreword

When the sons of Khalsa are called upon to face the enemy they do so with only one resolution in mind – to do the right thing at all cost. The morning of 12 Sept 1897 at Saragarhi saw such an example of pure grit and determination of the highest order.

It is an incredible story of 21 men of the 36th Sikh Regiment (currently 4th Sikh Regiment) who gave their lives in devotion to their duty; they all chose to fight until their last breath and they did so with the regimental battle cry of *"Jo Bole So Nihal, Sat Siri Akal"* (meaning: those who utter the Timeless God's praises are freed from all pains).

Under the command of Havildar (Sergeant) Ishar Singh, this signalling post saw some of the fiercest hand to hand combat between the highly decorated 21 men and an estimated 10,000 Afghan tribesmen in the North-West frontier. It highlights the actions of true heroes in a hostile unforgiving terrain, against all odds during the uprising of the turbulent Pathan tribes of Tirah.

On that morning, in overwhelming numbers, the tribes attacked the fort but met fierce resistance from the outnumbered Sikhs, who fought them back with such valour, inflicting heavy casualties on the offenders. For their unwavering bravery the soldiers were decorated posthumously with the Indian Order of Merit, the highest military award in India.

Sikh military and civilian personnel commemorate this battle every year, the day aptly named Saragarhi Day. It has been brought to life by the author and I thoroughly recommend reading it, the hair on the back of your neck will stand up. I salute those brave warriors whose sacrifices have laid a beautiful path for many to tread.

Sikhs are socially and economically vibrant across the globe in public and private sectors. The Sikh adherents founded in the 15th century, whilst small in numbers but big in heart, continue to have a significant impact on the global platform, encouraging the young blood to strive and achieve success.

The Sikh identity has become more understood and respected as the contribution of the faith is celebrated in all corners of the Earth.

This story is crucial to keeping the spirit of the Sikhs alive. It not only reminds us of the values and standards that need to be upheld in the highest esteem but also the need for selfless service (*seva*).

"He who serves will always be remembered"

Captain Makand Singh MBE
British Army

Preface

It's been ten years since I first heard about the story of Saragarhi from a friend who described it as a battle of epic proportions, on a par with the previous summer's blockbuster hit "300".

The latter was the well known story of how a group of three-hundred Spartans under King Leonidas fought to their deaths against Xerxes and the might of the Persian army at Thermopylae in 480 BC.

Saragarhi, on the other hand, was not well known to many beyond those who had read the history of the North West Frontier and the British Empire. It is the story of how twenty-one Sikh soldiers from the 36th (Sikh) Regiment of Bengal Infantry gallantly defended a small outpost for nearly seven hours during the onslaught of thousands of Afridi and Orakzai tribesmen. Faced with overwhelming odds the men fought until they died – not accepting surrender or the promise of safe passage should they lay down their arms.

But both Saragarhi and Thermopylae had many similarities: the battles pitted a small group of fighters against overwhelming odds. Both espoused the traditions of a warrior race. Both saw self-sacrifice of the men involved for a higher cause. Bravery, heroics, valour, courage, duty - all words used to describe the Sikhs and the Spartans.

To this we can also add some of the most renowned last stands in history to see how Saragarhi compares to popular battles in the public conscience:

During the siege at the Alamo in 1836, 189 poorly armed Texans faced upward of 2,000 Mexican troops. All were killed after lasting 13 days.

The Battle of Camaron in 1863 pitted 65 Frenchmen against 3,000 Mexican infantry and cavalrymen. Three men survived, cementing the reputation of the French Foreign Legion. At Rorke's Drift in 1879, 139 British cooks, supply clerks and engineers were surrounded by thousands of Zulu warriors and undertook a valiant defence despite wave after wave of attacks.

If Saragarhi is comparable to such last heroic stands then why is it not more widely recognised? Why has it been forgotten? My curiosity led me to enquire why it was not so well known outside of military circles, why no literature had delved into the story of the twenty-one or why no production had ever been made celebrating their heroics. Indeed where the story prevailed it was full of emotional sentiment and with little historic grounding which I felt meant the true essence and understanding of its impact then – and now – has been forgotten if not entirely lost.

Armed with these questions and concerns I immersed myself into reading everything I could about Saragarhi, about the Samana where the outpost was positioned, about the period of the "Great Game" when the battle took place, about the 36th Sikhs whose regiment it involved, about Lt Col John Haughton who commanded the men on the ridge and about the British attitude towards Sikhs.

On my quest for facts and information I started with simple online searches then expanded to delving into hidden archives at libraries and military establishments in Britain and India. Secondary accounts were investigated and primary resources sought. It was noted where they tallied, and any dissimilarity further analysed for clarification of what was made up or added to the story after the event.

The more I read about Saragarhi and the Samana the more it became apparent that this was a story worth telling in its wider historic context to a mainstream audience. Why did the tribes rise up in the region? Why were the Sikhs raised into a regiment and dispatched to fight them? How did the battle play out? What affects did it have on those who fought alongside them? And how was the heroic action received in Britain and India? All questions I wanted to find answers to.

More so when I found that there has developed alongside this forgotten battle many myths and mistruths about it, a sad reflection of what happens to historic events when they are not properly researched and documented or when proper records are not kept at libraries and military centres. This includes Saragarhi being listed as one of seven epic battles by UNESCO. Or that Saragarhi is taught in French military academies. And that news of the events at Saragarhi was received with applause in the British House of Commons...

While all sound fairly plausible, I found myself as a journalist questioning their truthfulness – MPs in the Commons do not applaud, and no record can be found of Saragarhi in Hansard; UNESCO representatives told me they knew nothing of the claims - and so I sought to prove the validity of these and other such stories with thorough research. Where I found no evidence or basis of fact such myths were rejected as baseless, but I remain open to being convinced if evidence of such can be presented.

I sought the hard truth of what Saragarhi represents today and why it had not received greater attention over the last century. In doing so I delved into the facts to find out whether what sounded like a truly remarkable episode in Anglo-Sikh history was as important as it seemed. Sifting through primary sources I sought to paint an accurate picture of the battle and its place in history, where accounts could not be verified I set them aside as part of the mythology that has taken root in the story. This includes references to signal messages sent from the post, which I could not find any primary example of but accept that verbal personal accounts might contain some reference to them.

In undertaking my research, my objective was to narrate the battle as factually as possible – the focus and fascination being on the Sikhs who had fought for the British Empire and what element of their psyche drove them to self-sacrifice for a Queen and Country they had never seen.

The story told here is about duty and sacrifice, tradition and honour, about the trust between the British and Sikhs and how this strong bond led to such gallant acts of valour which proved so crucial during the period of the "Great Game" played between Britain and Russia. It is my sincere wish that reading about this will inspire others to research further and deeper into this episode and other historic events at large.

The reason I want to tell it is because the story had meaning for the Sikhs and British in the immediate aftermath of the battle. It established the Sikhs as loyal and brave soldiers under British rule.

And it could be argued that the heroics displayed on the frontier led to greater dependency and deployment of Sikhs all over the Empire seventeen years later during the Great War.

By looking closely at the fighting spirit of the Sikhs back then, I believe the story can still be relevant for people in the 21st century in Britain, India and beyond. It should highlight Sikh values and the bravery and staunch nature of a race whose belief system has created a warrior-saint society that abides by truth, justice and selflessness.

And as long as they remain true to the religious tenets enshrined within the holy scriptures of Guru Granth Sahib, the Sikhs can continue to benefit from the blessings bestowed upon them by their Gurus.

Since I began my journey in telling this story we have achieved much in Britain to raise awareness of its significance to new audiences. The first edition of this book was launched in the Indian Army Memorial Room, Old College, Royal Military Academy Sandhurst in 2013. The event began an annual event hosted by Her Majesty's Armed Forces – the UK's official Saragarhi Day commemoration. As this book is republished in 2017, Saragarhi Day is now into its fifth year and being held at the National Memorial Arboretum in Staffordshire, the home of the WW1 Sikh Memorial. This

This work has also been spun off, with presentations being delivered up and down the country as well as abroad, recently at the prestigious

United Services Institute of Delhi and the Centre for Armed Forces Historical Research.

As we mark the prestigious 120th anniversary, I'm pleased that my long held ambition of producing a factual documentary about Saragarhi has also come to fruition – the new film will be released to mark the commemoration on Saragarhi Day, be screened on British television and will then be toured all over the world.

This inspirational story is one which should be open and accessible to all – and so this book updated for the 120th anniversary year of the battle includes facts and photographs sourced from primary sources, coupled with my knowledge and understanding of the Sikh psyche to give an accurate portrayal of the events which led to twenty-one brave men fighting to the bitter end for a foreign power in a land far away from their homes.

Telling this story as factually and historically accurate as possible would have been difficult still had it not been for the input and guidance of various specialists: my dear friend Harjinder Singh from Akaal Publishers who assisted with research and resources required to paint a picture of Saragarhi.

Many more are becoming aware of Saragarhi and there has been an increase in projects that bring this story to the fore, whether in comic books or film adaptations. While we continue to salute the endeavours of the brave Sikhs who fought on the Samana by remembering their heroics let us also do their story justice - by narrating historic fact as fact and delve into the lessons it has to offer to those willing to be inspired. This can bring some direction to how we live our lives today: with courage, conviction and unshakeable commitment to the words and teachings of the Sikh Gurus.

Capt. J. Singh-Sohal
British Library, 2017

Maps

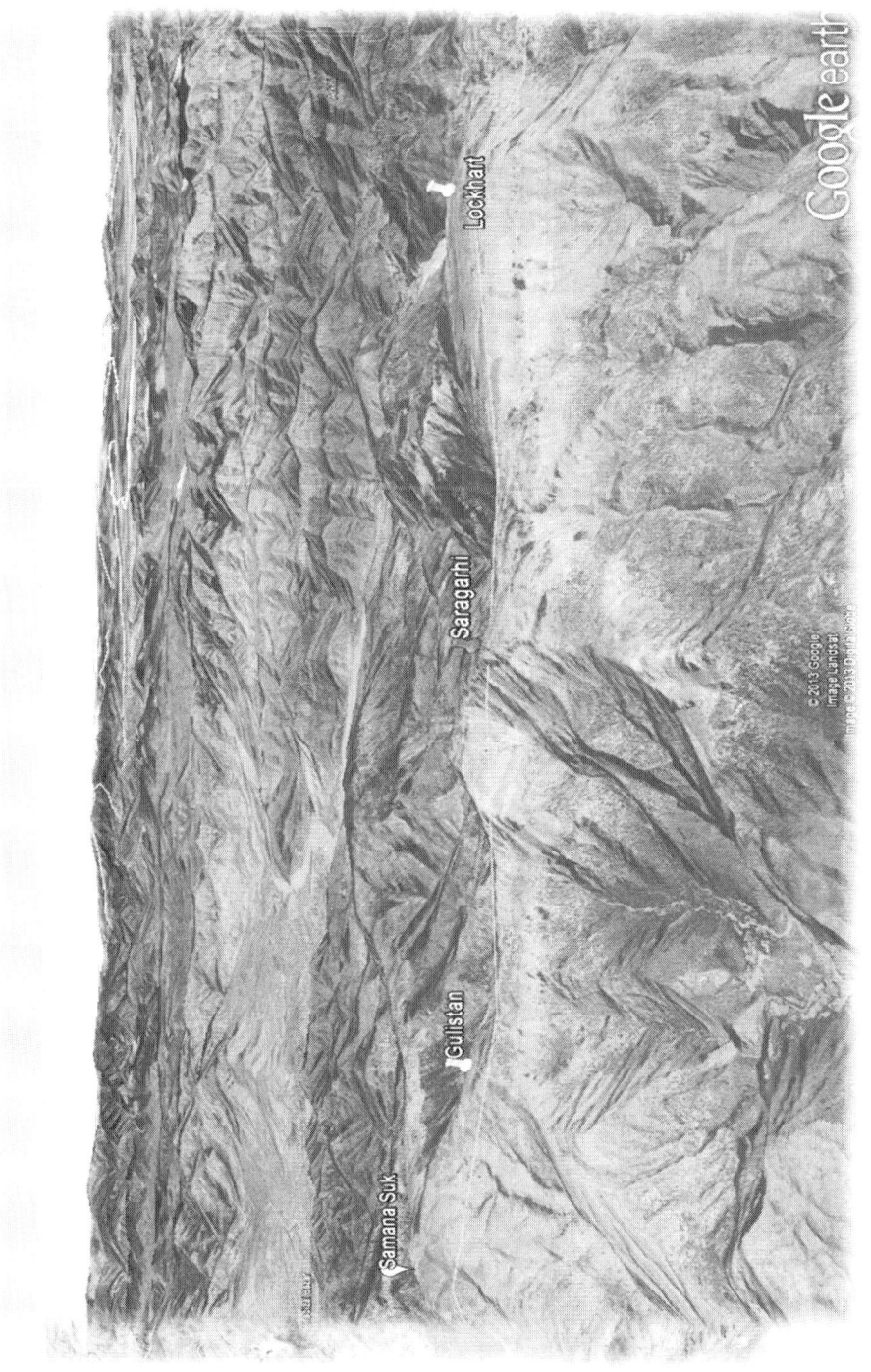

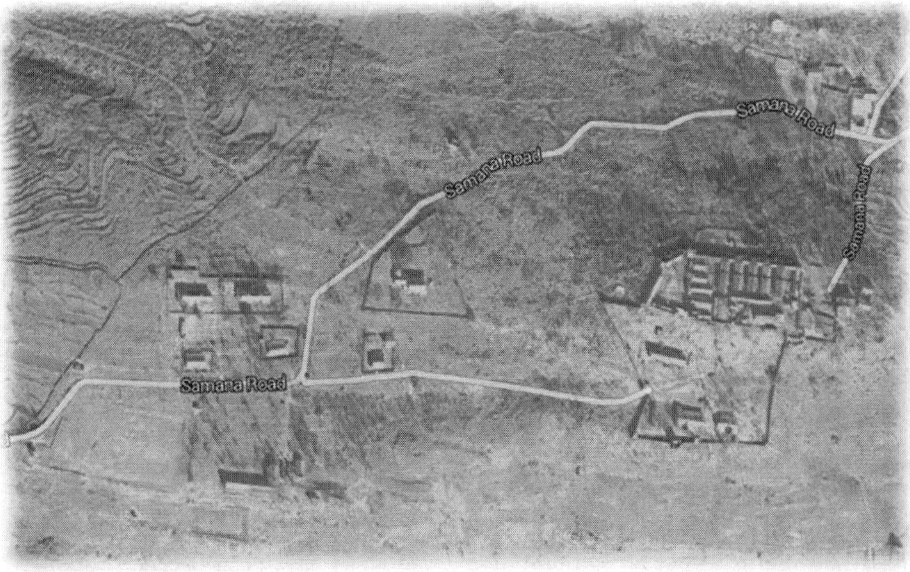
Samana Road
Samana Road
Samana Road
Samana Road

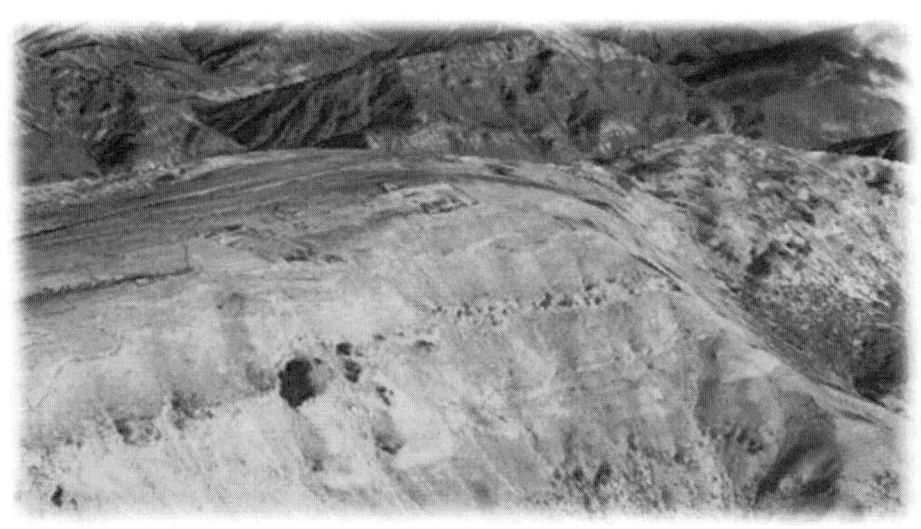

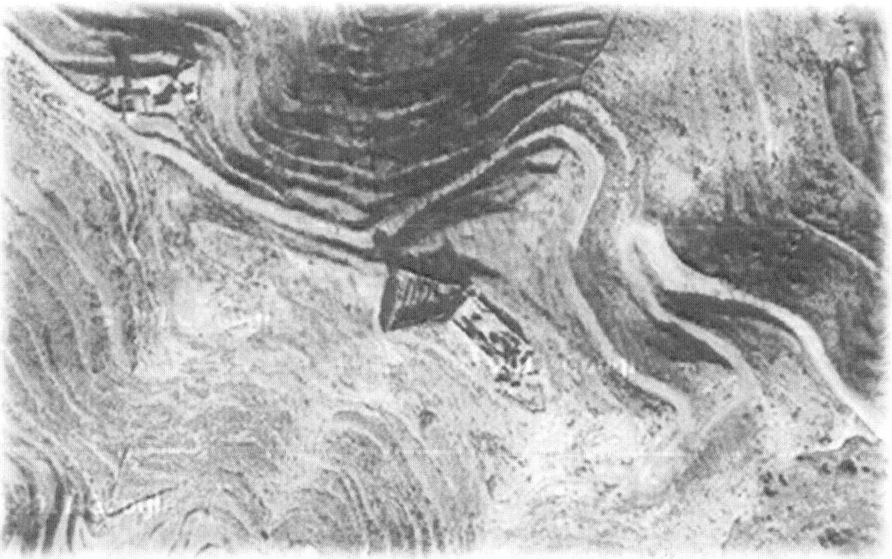

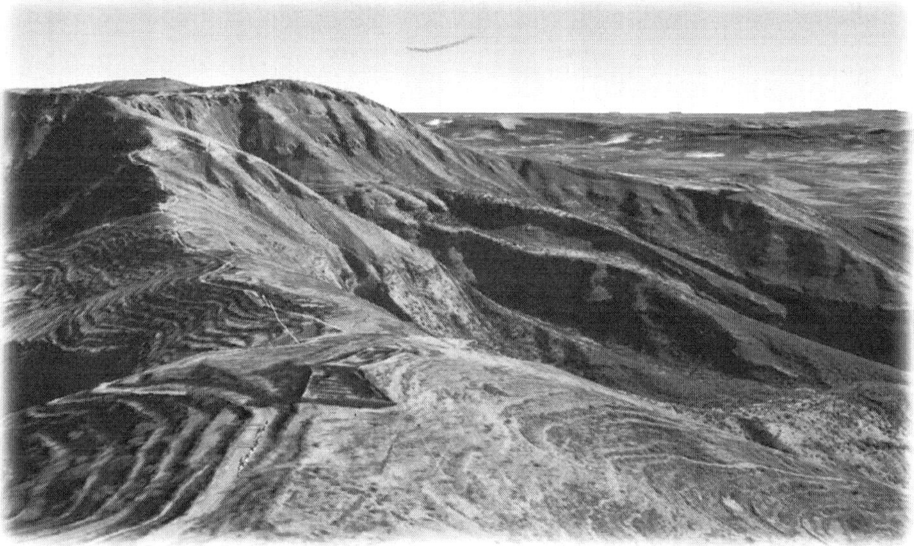

Above: the only surviving photograph of Saragarhi outpost, as seen from Fort Lockhart in 1897, before it was destroyed on 12th September.

Above: Saragarhi in the far right as seen from Fort Gulistan
Below: The surrounding tribal country on the Samana

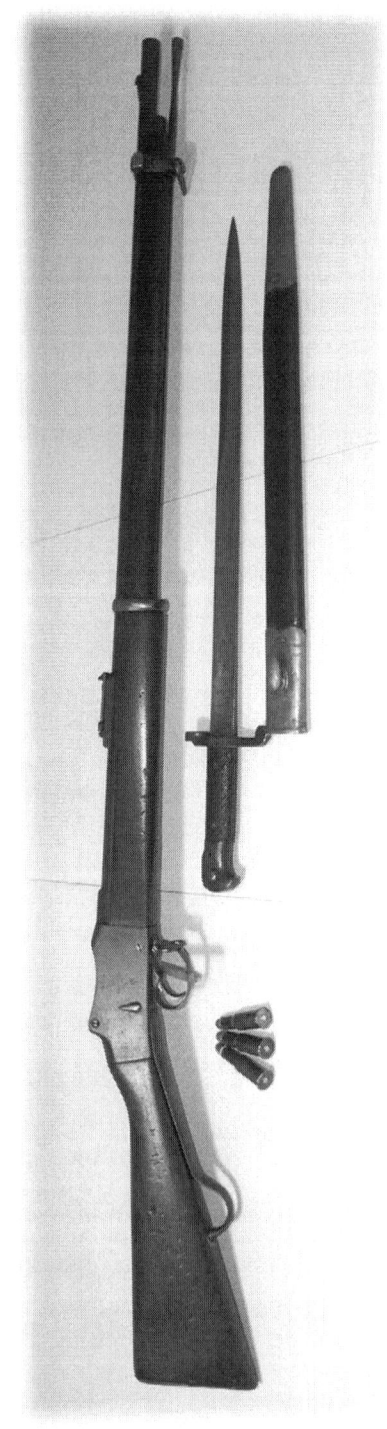

The Martini Henry mk IV and bayonet as used by the 36th Sikhs on the North West frontier.

Introduction

The site of Saragarhi today is in the Khyber Pakhtunkhwa region of Pakistan. Situated west of the district capital Kohat, the small communications post took its name from the nearby Pathan village that previously existed at its site.

The Samana area where the British built the forts and posts defended by the 36th Sikhs is now largely inaccessible to tourists and foreigners due to the close proximity to the border with Afghanistan and the danger that brings. The Pakistan military still operates out of the old Fort Lockhart site, now called Fort Samana, and the area surrounding it forms part of the cantonment, a military controlled area, within which area filming and photography is also strictly prohibited.

The Pakistan military still undertakes active operations against Islamist militants in the tribal areas including Samana, and armed check posts are positioned on the entrance into the cantonment making it further difficult for even local people to more around freely.

But should one be lucky to venture out to the Samana ridge amongst the green hills and sparse villages that in humid summer months provide scenes of natural beauty; one would find two old forts called Lockhart and Gulistan, which men from British and native Indian regiments defended during the period of Empire and in the "Great Game" against Russia.

Lockhart lies about nine and Gulistan twelve miles west of the town of Hangu, which itself was an important post situated about twenty-five miles west of the town of Kohat. And it was the close proximity to the latter that gave the mountainous Samana its strategic importance. Kohat was a major garrison town for the British during the Raj and provided a base of operations into the Khyber and tribal areas, particularly Tirah in the North-West.

Home to the Afridi, Orakzai and Shinwari tribes of Pashtun, Tirah lies deep within the mountain ranges in a sort of cul-de-sac accessible only by one of five mountainous passes. This includes the Sampagha Pass, near the Khanki Valley which is itself north of the Samana. Because of its enclosed nature, Tirah had not been touched by the first two Anglo-Afghan Wars nor visited by any foreign visitor – a false sense of security that contributed to various tribal uprisings in the 1890's.

This is important to note, as it is because of the context of other larger expeditions and actions against the Pathan tribes that the events at Saragarhi can be seen to have been lost within history. Nonetheless, it is still remembered within military circles as one of the greatest last stands.

In telling the true story of Saragarhi it is necessary to give the bigger picture of the context to the battle and what occurred before and during it on the Samana range. With this knowledge the reasons for the events of 1897 can be better understood – and greater emphasis placed on the significance of the heroic actions at Saragarhi, Gulistan and Lockhart by a people who had once fought against the very Empire they were now defending.

As such, this volume begins with the period of history in which it took place, the "Great Game", itself a fascinating episode worthy of further exploration. Providing the context of this and why the British Indian Army was engaged in frontier wars gives the basis of appreciating their importance in defending India from foreign threat at this time.

A closer look is then taken at the Samana range and the military actions which brought it under British control. Whilst not entirely delving away from Saragarhi, knowing of the region and geography provides vital insight into the positioning and nature of the outposts which have only to date been found in contemporary records of the period. It is through this that we get to see where Saragarhi was and what the post looked like– with official records and a rare photo of it that has with this research come to light and is published here for the first time.

Turning then to the Sikhs themselves, an introduction to the faith is necessary, to provide the basis of understanding of their martial spirit from the founding of the faith by the first Guru Nanak Dev to the establishment of the Khalsa creed under the tenth Guru Gobind Singh.

Sikhs are a unique and distinct race whose history and belief system has evolved through battle. Sikhs pride themselves on their independence, but at some time this changed and allegiance was sworn to the British. The reasons why are explored, and then the relationship between the two is further investigated to show the mutual respect garnered between them which would prove momentous in world conflicts.

Then on to the regiment of Saragarhi, the 36th Sikhs, their founding and early deployments are given to narrate how they found themselves on the frontier. Details are also given of how they were raised, about their commanding officer and some background on some of the soldiers who would serve at the outpost. This is followed by the nature of the tribal uprising which led to the events of 1897.

Turning to the events on the Samana itself, the narrative history of the conflict is given using primary and contemporary sources. The action at Gulistan and Lockhart is described as well as at Saragarhi to give a fuller picture of the battle. Then a brief look at the 36th Sikhs during the Tirah campaign follows to complete the story of their deployment on the frontier and what would lead to a dark day for the regiment with the death of their heroic commander.

The historic event provides a tale of modern inspiration, and so the significance of the battle and why it is an important episode of British and Sikh history is then shown through contemporary press accounts, letters and speeches. The ways in which Sikhs were given recognition by their superiors is described as well as the rewards they received for their service, such as the Samana bar on the India General Service medal and for those who exhibited bravery the Indian Order of Merit.

The remembrance of Saragarhi thereafter forms a crucial chapter, as the enduring memory of the battle and those who fought is one which this volume seeks to promote. Looking at the various ways in which Saragarhi is remembered in India and abroad should show that this battle which has been forgotten by much of the world still has a place in the Indian psyche.

And the legacy of the battle is given in relation to significance of the Sikh contribution on the frontier and what it meant heading into the Great War. The importance cannot be overstated for the latter, as Sikhs proved themselves worthy of serving in every area of the conflict the British were involved in.

By the conclusion, it will be seen how the factual nature of Saragarhi has been forgotten and instead how the battle has taken on a mythical status. In drawing together the research, it will be shown that the historical facts surrounding events on the Samana give better understanding to why Sikhs did what they did – and how their actions can continue to inspire people today.

In researching and laying forth the story of Saragarhi in its wider context, no doubt some gaps in knowledge and understanding might appear. While every pain has been taken to give the full picture, some areas require further exploration – particularly more about the soldiers themselves and their life stories before and during their service in British India. I would be grateful for any such information to evolve this work into the comprehensive history of the event which it seeks to be.

The "Great Game"

The region of the North West Frontier was unruly but at the fore of British policy during the height of Empire in the mid to late 19th century. It was during the so called "Great Game" with Imperial Russia that Britain fought to maintain control over it.

This was a period of strategic rivalry between both empires over control of Central Asia and began when the Russians signed a treaty of peace with Persia at Gulistan (a village in modern day Azerbaijan) which gave them free reign over a large landmass that included modern day Georgia, Dagestan, and areas neighbouring Afghanistan.

With this Russia set its sights on the wealth of the sub-continent, Britain was alarmed and so manoeuvred to maintain its hold over India and prevent Afghanistan being used as a staging post or thoroughfare for an invasion.

The heightened tensions of the time saw the first Anglo-Afghan war in 1839 when the British tried to exert control over Afghanistan by occupying Kabul; but failed to check an insurgency and were forced to make a disastrous retreat at the cost of thousands of lives.

It was followed by a second war in 1878 which finally led to British superiority in the country through diplomacy and the threat of aggression. Internal politics was left to the Amir of Afghanistan, but Britain controlled the country's foreign policy. The Khyber Pass was crucial to trade and so re-opened in February 1881[1].

But more important than its commercial value was its strategic significance in the event of military intervention in Afghanistan. Tribesmen were paid off to ensure they stopped raiding baggage trains travelling through it. The British had found that raising local levies to police the Khyber was a cheaper and more effective tactic in checking tribal attacks, although the danger was these forces could not be relied upon when conflict did break out against their kinsmen.

But the Russians continued to penetrate eastwards in Turkestan[2]and demanded the re-bordering of frontiers with Afghanistan, seizing the north-western town of Panjdeh in 1885. To avoid all out war, a compromise was reached two years later and on the Indian side a Boundary Commission set up with agreement from the Amir of Afghanistan to finally define spheres of British and Afghan influence[3].

Britain now developed a "forward policy" of occupying frontier lands and keeping a presence in places inhabited by Pathans which they sought to influence in order to maintain security. Sikhs were once again called upon in great numbers to protect India on the frontier and would be raised into regiments whose sole purpose was to serve there against any emerging threat.

In 1891, Brigadier General Sir William Lockhart led two expeditions of the Miranzai Field Force onto the Samana range in order to bring the tribes there under control.

The first expedition was launched in January of that year to search for positions to build forts on the mountain, the building of which was postponed until the snow had cleared away[4].

By the 11th February 1891, the village of Saragarhi had come to the attention of the expedition and the 1st Column of the Miranzai Field Force. The column was led by Colonel Andrew Murison McCrae Bruce.

Born in 1842, Bruce was commissioned at the age of eighteen and served in India with the 2nd Bengal Fusiliers, 1st Gurkhas and 4th Punjab Infantry. By the time of the Miranzai expedition he was already experienced on the frontier and had fought during the second Afghan war of 1879-80.

Leading the 4th Punjab Infantry he marched with 150 rifles to the Mastan plateau and occupied the area which was in a strategic position[5]. They left the next day to clear nearby towers in the area, which enemy sharp shooters could have used against the encroaching British and Indians. After some bloodshed the first Miranzai expedition was hailed a success and the clans accepted, with some reluctance, the location of posts and construction of roads on the Samana[6].

But this would quickly spill into more conflict with the tribes in the area once again rising up. In March 1891, villagers in Tsangai attacked Sikh troops stationed there. Noteworthy in official records are the heroics of Sepoy Diwan Singh who *"displayed great gallantry"* in defending one of his wounded men and in keeping the enemy at bay until reinforcements arrived, while another soldier Sepoy Jaimal Singh *"exhibited the dogged courage of the Sikh in carrying off under heavy fire"* the body of his cohort Sepoy Rur Singh who had been killed[7]. Both men were subsequently rewarded the Indian Order of Merit (the highest award then possible for them) for their gallant conduct.

A month later and on the morning of 20th April the enemy had assembled around the villages of Saragarhi which were attacked by the 5th Gurkha Regiment and the King's Royal Rifles. It was reported that the enemy whittled away with heavy losses[8]. The official military records of that expedition state that five towers were blown up and five hamlets destroyed. Enemy losses amounted to 300 killed or wounded, while the British lost 2 and had 6 wounded[9].

The policy of occupying enemy ground was proving useful for the British on the frontier; whole villages were entirely cleared away so that the Pathans had no presence on the Samana[10]. These were nearly all in ruins anyway after the Miranzai expedition which made it simpler for frontier fortifications to be erected. These would ensure control over the area and the tribes living there – as well as keep the Russians at arm's length from British India.

The Samana

Finding the area strategically important, the British took to strengthening their position on the Samana. A memorandum was issued in May 1891 on the posts and roads that were to be created for the military occupation of the range. Within it, the Commander-in-Chief of India, General Sir Frederick Roberts (who months later became Baron Roberts of Kandahar) approved the building of several structures which would prove vital in later conflicts with the Pathans. The main structures were positioned on high ground and on through-routes to make the best use of the terrain.

The high point at Gulistan, at 6,152 feet, was manned by 200 men; one company would be housed in a post on the site of the village of the same name while another company (including two officers) would be lodged in huts on the small hill to the west. This was done to avoid greater expense and delay in its construction.

The memo notes that the huts were *"to be surrounded by strong stone parapets with ditches outside, and to be connected by a covered way with the main work or keep. The western face of the enclosure should be on the crest of the hill, and the flanks falling towards the rear will be defiladed by the western parapet.*[11]*"*

Gulistan was also known as Fort Cavagnari, after Major Sir Pierre Louis Napoleon Cavagnari an Anglo-Frenchman whose father had served as one of Napoleon's generals. Cavagnari had negotiated and signed the Treaty of Gandamak which created a post of British representative to Kabul that he took up in 1879.

On the nearby Mastan plateau, at a height of 6,496 feet, was built the larger main post to garrison two-and-a-half companies or around 300 men. It provided quarters for four officers and would be the headquarters for the battalion occupying the Samana[12].

Again, the Mastan post was renamed after a British officer – this time General Sir William Lockhart who was Road Commandant of the Khyber Pass, had served in the Second Afghan War and was no stranger to the Samana having led the expedition that recaptured the area in the expedition of 1891. General Lockhart would also return to the area after the events of 1897 to lead the Tirah Expeditionary Force, and it is to him that leading Sikh Sardar's wrote to express their solidarity with the British months after the events of Saragarhi.

While the main post was placed on the highest part of the plateau, two small picquet posts would be placed elsewhere at the "Crag" picquet hill to the north and another on the high part of the main range west of the village of Saragarhi at 6,200 feet. *"The latter post will be visible both from Mastan and Gulistan[13]"* says the memorandum, giving some indication of its strategic importance (detailed later).

To warn against an enemy advance in the area, simple and inexpensive picquet posts were also situated nearby at Dhar, Sartop and Sangar. These, as Saragarhi, were built to accommodate a garrison of twenty-five to fifty men[14]. If properly maintained each post could stand a siege for up to thirty-seven hours[15].

Posts at Lakha, Tsalai, Gogra and Saifaldara completed the enclosure around the area and were held by the border military police and tribal levies[16] made up of local Pathans who were paid to defend them against their kinsmen.

The Commander-in-Chief's memo goes further into the construction of the posts, which gives some idea of how Saragarhi might have been built. It notes that what was required from the posts was *"simply dry stone rectangular enclosures with flanking bastions at the opposite diagonal corners"* with barracks for troops and a guard room and that *"all posts must be provided with iron water tanks for storage of water.[17]"*

The height of the posts is given particular attention, with nine feet *"sufficient extreme height for the interior of the barracks which, allowing*

1 foot for the thickness of roof covering, and a 4 feet parapet, gives a total height of 14 feet to the walls. " Furthermore *"iron roofs are considered undesirable, as the heat of the sun in the day time is very great, besides which the slopes given to such roofs entail unnecessary complications and expense with consequent delay in the constructions of the banquettes.*[18]*"*

The main posts at Gulistan and Lockhart *"should each be provided with two rifle calibre machine guns on parapet mountings. The bastions should have faces about twenty feet long and flanks projecting ten feet to provide for a suitable number of flanking rifles.*[19]*"*

Saragarhi post was situated about a mile and a half west of Lockhart and a mile and three-quarters east of Gulistan[20]. By analysing a photo of Saragarhi from before it was destroyed, it can be seen that the outpost comprised a tower on the south side facing the cliff drop with covered breastworks around the other sides to give the soldiers positioned there a raised platform to fire from. There is also a guard room and a two-storey building, possibly as sleeping quarters. (See image).

It was considered the most important of these minor forts because through it heliographic signal communications could be maintained between Lockhart and Gulistan, and thus control over the Samana range[21].While the telegraph had been invented much earlier in 1832 by Samuel Morse, the heliograph became a necessary means of sending Morse code on the frontier.

Field telegraphs had been put up between Gulistan and Lockhart but the wire laid beneath the ground to carry these messages kept being cut by the locals[22]. When they were repaired the enemy persevered, so it became necessary for another means of sending messages to be deployed.

The heliograph sent Morse code through the use of flashing lights. Its simplicity and ease of use meant it became popular in British India as an effective means of communication[23]. The main helio artery on the frontier was the Peshawar to Kabul link which consisted of twenty stations covering 180 miles[24]. Its use is best demonstrated in a Times newspaper report published the morning after the battle of Ahmedkhel in 1880, which was telephoned up to the helio station on a hillside and transmitted by heliograph signal from the field to a junction station, from where it was telegraphed back to London[25].

It was with this novel means of communication in a mountainous area not easily traversed that the Sikhs ventured into at a time when British India faced threats from the big bear of Europe, Russia.

But why did the Sikhs fight the way they did, and in what manner had their faith and belief in the words of their True Guru inspired them to do so for a foreign superpower?

To understand the psyche of the Sikhs we must turn to their creation.

The Sikh Martial Spirit

The Sikh faith was founded by the first Guru Nanak Dev in 1469. The fledging faith spread a simple message of living in accordance with the Will of God.

The followers of Guru Nanak were encouraged to recite the name of God, earn an honest living and share their earnings and success with those less fortunate. Material wealth mattered little to achieving realisation of the Lord, a path which was open to all regardless of sex, class or creed.

The faith had peaceful roots but was by no means a pacifistic movement. Guru Nanak challenged the ritualistic lifestyles of people from all walks of life. The Guru took to debate and discourse in his fight to eradicate such social ills as caste prejudice, female discrimination and superstitions about religion and God.

The message Guru Nanak conveyed was that God could be found in all of creation – so why undertake pointless penances and actions when what was needed was sincere devotion.

In spreading this message, the Guru travelled far and wide and spoke to all people about living with Godly virtue; tours all over India, the Middle East and parts of Africa in the west and China in the east are well documented but no doubt the Guru also visited many more places.

Guru Nanak roused the spirit of those he met, showing the light of salvation to all from the highest rulers to the lowest dregs of society. The Mughal ruler Babar humbly came to the Guru's court, the renowned cannibal Kauda Rakkash and serial killer Sajjan Tag changed their ways after meeting the Guru. Such was the enlightening presence of the Guru that his message changed people for the better.

The qualities that made the followers of Guru Nanak unique were the staunch belief in his words and teachings, commands which had been passed to the Guru by God himself. The disciple was constantly learning and evolving in order to reach greater spiritual heights. They became known as "Sikh" which in Persian means one ever willing to learn.

Guru Nanak preached to his followers that only through controlling the mind could they become champions of the physical world. Lust, anger, greed, attachment and ego were all to be checked through voluntary service, prayer and a life of virtue. Sikhs thus developed   a spirit of self-respect, restraint and control, discipline and humility which would evolve to become a part of their warrior code.

The Guru's message was further developed by nine successive living Gurus, but the martyrdom of the fifth Guru Arjan Dev at the hands of the Mughal's had a profound effect. The Guru had accepted martyrdom in order to protect the sanctity of the Ad Granth, the compilation of scriptures which the Guru himself bowed down to.

The freedom of speech and expression Sikhs sought through the word of their Guru now needed teeth, as the need arose to protect the mainstay of Sikh identity through a martial renaissance it would be tempered with steel.

Guru Arjan Dev's son, Hargobind, became the sixth Guru in 1606 and began to form the Sikh community into a nation through their militarisation. The Guru himself took to wearing two swords over each shoulder to signify the merger of spirituality, *piri,* with a new martial tradition, *miri*, amongst Sikhs[26].

The Guru instructed his Sikhs to carry weapons at all times and trained them to become warriors. Sikhs would exert the use of force when all peaceful and diplomatic means had failed. The Guru thus created a military ethos amongst the Sikhs which was needed to defend the principles of the faith against growing external threats[27].

This policy set up a clash with the Mughal's under Emperor Jahangir, who decreed that only Muslims could carry weapons. The Guru went further and in 1608 built a throne, the *Akal Takht,* opposite the *Harimandir Sahib* in Amritsar from which he issued political commands to his followers.

Guru Hargobind was the first Guru to engage in open battle against the regime. These battles were all defensive in nature; seven were fought between 1628 and 1635. The Guru's standing army consisted of 700 cavalrymen, sixty gunners and 500 infantrymen and effectively created a state-within-a-state; but the use of military means was always the last resort to resolving conflict. When Jahangir ordered the Guru be imprisoned at a fort in Gwalior, the Guru voluntarily came forward and later through diplomacy secured his own release and that of fifty-two other kings who were imprisoned[28].

Subsequent Guru's maintained the Sikh army and call to arms, but the tenth Guru Gobind Rai was instructed by Divine Will to cement it as a core principle of the Khalsa brotherhood of initiated Sikhs. Once again, it was with the martyrdom of his father – and ninth Guru – that Guru Gobind took up the sword for a Sikh renaissance.

The Guru knew full well that the Sikhs were at heart peace loving people with no spark of self-assertion or retaliation in their hearts. The message of Guru Nanak was well embedded within the community but followers were not well endowed in martial confidence to pick up weapons and be formidable in appearance so as to evoke fear and awe[29].

In 1699 the Guru changed this and created a warrior-saint creed which would defy any worldly power set against it. Appearing dressed in his warrior garbs and with sword in hand at the Vaisakhi festival in Anandpur, the Guru asked for loyal devotees to give him their heads.

Five men from various castes stepped forward to offer their lives, and the Guru initiated them into the Khalsa by administering *amrit,* or nectar stirred in an iron bowl with a double-edged sword while prayers were recited.

They became the *panj pyare,* or five beloved ones, and adopted the dress code of a martial warrior race - growing their hair long and wearing turbans on their heads. Their surname became Singh meaning lion, which did away with class distinctions but also underlined their warlike nature as warriors[30].

From here on *kes*, or unshorn hair, became compulsory for any Sikh who took initiation and it was a cardinal sin to cut ones hair. The Khalsa would also keep with them the five k's, symbols of faith which had spiritual and practical uses. As well as the uncut hair they also included: *kara* or iron bracelet, *kaccherra* or knee-length briefs, *kirpan* or short dagger, *kangha* or wooden comb. Initiates were also to stand forth in turbans which would make them at once recognisable as the Guru's disciples[31].

The Guru himself then kneeled before the five and asked for initiation – becoming Guru Gobind Singh. The Khalsa was given a place of superiority in Sikhdom, equal to the scriptures which would become the Guru Granth Sahib. Five Khalsa initiates would forever represent the Guru in form in any decision made for the good of the faith and wherever they went.

In describing the high status of the Khalsa, the Guru wrote in the *Sarbloh Granth* that the brotherhoods insignia is honour and greatness, adding:

Khalsa is my source of strength.
Khalsa is my body and breath.
Khalsa is my duty and destiny.

And to give insight into the greatness of the Khalsa that:

Khalsa is the Immortal Being's militia.
Creation of the Khalsa is the Supreme Being's Will.

After the creation of the Khalsa in 1699, Guru Gobind Singh continued to direct the Sikhs in how to live their lives and issued edicts and instructions on how the Khalsa should behave. Battles were fought with the Mughal's and Hindu Hill Raja's because of the Khalsa's gaining wealth, power and supremacy.

The Khalsa showed its willingness to fight to the last for what it believed in, particularly at the battle of Chamkaur in 1704 where a million Mughal's surrounded and faced off against the Guru and forty-seven Sikhs. These included his two elder sons Sahibzada's Ajit Singh and Jujhar Singh who asked permission to attack the enemy and were martyred. Outnumbered, five Sikhs gave an edict to the Guru to escape – and created a distraction by engaging the enemy in small bands of five or six overnight. The next day the Mughal's stormed the small mud fort of Chamkaur and the remaining Sikhs inside were killed.

Such heroic last stands were continued by the Sikhs, who embraced martyrdom in this way rather than surrender their faith or identity to the enemy. But for every Sikh that was killed more would take his place and join the Khalsa.

But the issue of sovereignty was one the Sikhs would struggle with over the next century, as the Guru left for his heavenly abode in 1708. With his passing, the line of living Gurus came to an end but the mission started by Guru Nanak would continue to be fulfilled by the Khalsa.

So if the Sikh psyche was embedded with a strong sense of independence and sovereignty, then why did they yield to a foreign super power?

To understand this we must turn to the fall of the second Sikh Empire and how British imperial policy favoured the Sikhs.

The Anglo-Sikh Relationship

There has historically been a strong connection between Great Britain and the Sikh nation going back to the reign of "the lion of the Punjab" Maharaja Ranjit Singh who had carved out an empire that spread from the frontier with Afghanistan to the outskirts of Delhi. The ruler had consolidated the Sikh misls and conquered Lahore in 1801 and Kashmir in 1819. The British recognised this power base in the North-West of India and entered into a friendship with Ranjit Singh.

But with the death of the Maharaja the *Sarkar* or government fell apart with various factions vying for control over the crown and looking to benefit from the ensuing chaos. These led the empire into the Anglo-Sikh Wars, where during the Sutlej campaign in 1845-6 and the Punjab campaign in 1848-9, the British found the Sikhs to be brave, and heroic on the battlefield. Despite the treachery of their Dogra commanders, the Sikhs fought against the British to the bitter end of defeat and earned a reputation as fearsome in the process.

The Sikhs were a broken people, because of the manner in which the Punjab was subjugated, who found themselves devoid of the land their leaders had struggled and died to protect and make their own. Without the freedom to express their martial tradition and with Christian missionaries active in the Punjab, it was feared in some quarters that Sikhs would merge into the predominant Hindu fold. But there was some unlikely aid from British quarters as the victors decided to harness the fighting power and determination of the Khalsa armies by raising the defeated units into a frontier force to send to the troublesome border with Afghanistan.

A small irregular body called the Trans-frontier Brigade was first created by Sir Henry Lawrence in May 1849. The force originally consisted of six infantry regiments and five cavalry, as well as an artillery unit. Four Sikh regiments came from the disbanded units of Sikhs after the Anglo-Sikh Wars, and were called the Regiments of Sikh Local Infantry. But in 1851 these became part of the new Punjab Irregular Force (or PIF) to serve on the frontier (and later in Burma and in Central India as well).

On 19th September 1865 the units were reorganised again into the Punjab Frontier Force, consisting of the 1st, 2nd (Hill), 3rd and 4th Regiment of Sikh Infantry; alongside four cavalry and five infantry units made up of the various castes and religions in the Punjab (see Appendix A). These would remain for much of the period of the "Great Game" until further reorganisation in 1903.

The British utilised the Sikhs in this way for two reasons, to keep them out of trouble in the Punjab and to deploy their fighting prowess against an old enemy, the Pathans. The British were well versed in Sikh faith and history and knew that the opportunity for Sikhs to fight against a people who had invaded the Punjab so often and harassed the Sikhs because of their distinct beliefs would appeal for many. One official found that these recruits *"take service readily and make excellent soldiers.[32]"* For some this presented a stable job opportunity during uncertain times. Others saw it as an adventure, rekindling memories of past heroes who had fought the Pathans such as Nawab Kapur Singh or Jassa Singh Ahluwalia.

Second Lieutenant Winston Churchill observed this during the Malakand campaign in July 1897, writing that: *"The Sikh is the guardian of the Marches. He was originally invented to combat the Pathan. His religion was designed to be diametrically opposed to Mahommedanism. It was a shrewd act of policy. Fanaticism was met by fanaticism. Religious abhorrence was added to racial hatred. The Pathan invaders were rolled back to the mountains and the Sikhs established themselves at Lahore and Peshawar[33]."*

In the 19th century the Sikhs were constantly fighting guerrilla warfare against the invading hordes of Ahmed Shah Abdali, founder of the Durrani dynasty. With their homeland sandwiched between the decaying Mughal's in Delhi and plundering Afghans in Kabul, the Sikhs lived in bands of fighters, or misls, who harassed both enemies whenever possible. Successfully fighting and defending their home turf, the Sikhs eventually became the masters of the Punjab and the once independent bands were absorbed into the Sukherchakia misl which had at its head Ranjit Singh.

The interaction between the Sikhs and Afghanistan under the direction of the British continued after the fall of the Sikh Empire in 1847, but it took the India Mutiny in 1857 to establish real trust and respect between the British and Sikhs.

Trouble began when native units within the Bengal Army mutinied; of the 148 major infantry and cavalry units only 55 remained loyal while others were disarmed or disbanded because they were likely to mutiny[34]. In the Punjab, the 11 infantry battalions and all six cavalry regiments, including all Sikh ones, remained loyal[35].

This had a dramatic effect on British India, with the East India Company being nationalised and all its possessions transferred to the Crown. The Indian Army was reorganised, with those units that remained loyal being rewarded and those that had mutinied disbanded and the gaps filled by regiments being raised by the loyal Sikhs and Punjabi's[36].

During the examination of why the mutiny had occurred, a theory developed about the "martial races" of India and why certain classes had not remained loyal. The Bengal Army that had mutinied had mainly comprised high-caste Brahmins from the plains who had problems with their dietary needs and did not serve alongside men of lower castes.

The Gurkha's and Sikhs had none of these social issues, were seen as naturally tall, well built and brave. This theory of who was a natural warrior inclined to accept the harsh realities of what war might mean to their lifestyles, and more importantly who wasn't, went some way in explaining for the British why mutiny occurred.

The British subsequently adapted their recruitment policies, and soon the Punjab became the cradle of the Indian Army[37] with the new Indian army comprising not just the Sikhs but the other tribes that were to be found in the land of five rivers – the Dogras, the Jatts (Hindu Kshatriya) and the Punjabi Mussalmans (Muslims).

The British view of a special martial race chimed with the Sikhs for whom this was simply an echo of what their Guru's had taught them about their faith and standing in the world. The Indian Army during British rule recruited many Sikhs – particularly Jatt farmers (who made up the majority of rural Punjab) whose profession of tilling the fields made them naturally stronger and bulkier, but even then recruitment officers insisted on enlisting the right type[38].

These were the initiated, or *amritdhari* Sikhs, who had accepted the discipline of the Khalsa and swore to abide by its code. The British respected and admired the virtue and spirit that this disciplined lifestyle instilled in them and sought to harness its power for their own cause – one that Sikhs wholeheartedly accepted.

Their faith and belief in God and Guru gave the Sikhs discipline and courage but British rule gave many purpose, and crucially, income. Raw recruits who stepped forward to join the military ranks were told to become initiated into the Khalsa first; those that did through the Army also swore an oath of loyalty to the Crown during the initiation ceremony.

In return, the British developed a special respect for Sikhs, one which went far beyond any recognition given by the British to a native race in their employment or Empire. Sikhs were allowed to observe the customs and traditions of their faith and encouraged to maintain the high standards of their belief system. Not even the Gurkha's, highly respected for their fighting ability, were accommodated in this way. It was said that, but for the Army, the Sikhs would have merged into Hinduism[39].

The Sikhs too stood out from their Pathan counterparts for their loyalty and dedication. The British had raised some Afghan tribal levies to police some posts along the frontier and in the Khyber, but were small in number as the tribesmen's loyalties lay stronger with their kinsmen. The Sikhs, in contrast, held a special place in frontier policy because of their past rivalry with the Pathans and were more respected for being better servants of the British.

Winston Churchill compared the soldierly virtues of the Sikhs and Pathans writing after Malakand that: *"In the Sikh the more civilised man appears. He does not shoot naturally, but he learns by patient practice. He is not tough as the Pathan, but he delights in feats of strength – wrestling, running or swimming.[40]"*

And in drawing on the importance that a Sikh soldier makes on the frontier, Churchill concludes: *"There are some who say that the Sikh will go on under circumstances which will dishearten and discourage his rival[41]"*- words that would ring true at Saragarhi.

By the turn of the 20th century Sikhs would prove with blood and valour that their race would stand shoulder to shoulder with the British – a fact which would not be forgotten in the largest conflict of its kind at the time, the Great War. But first the Sikhs had to earn their spurs.

They would do so on the Samana through their individual bravery and sacrifice.

The 36th Sikhs

With fears of Russia's growing sphere of influence and the thought of Afghanistan being used as a staging post for an invasion of India, during the so called "Great Game"; Britain moved to protect her interests by raising two new regiments to serve on the frontier.

The Sikhs already had a reputation for bravery and loyalty, so it was an ideal choice to create regiments containing their class with the purpose of being deployed to near Afghanistan to deal with any threat coming from the unruly region. It would also check the unruly Pathan tribes who had kept an uneasy truce after the Second Afghan War in 1878.

The 36th (Sikh) Regiment of Bengal Infantry was thus raised on 23rd March 1887 in Jullundur[42]. The regiment took its number designation from the Bareilly Levy which was raised in 1858 and went through several transformations in the run up to the second Afghan War 1878-80 but was disbanded in 1882.

The regiment was sister to the 35th Sikhs, both were raised disbanded and re-formed in the same manner. Both also shared the same formal uniform, red with yellow facings; as well as the same regimental centre in Rawalpindi.

The 36th consisted of 8 companies. 225 men were drafted in from twenty other infantry units of the Bengal Army and Punjab Frontier Force[43] to make up the new regiment while others were recruited from across Punjab. From May 1887 men were specifically recruited in the towns of Amritsar, Ferozepur, Gurdaspur, Hoshiaspur, Jullundur, Lahore, Ludhiana, Nabha and Patiala[44].

The Sikhs who made up both regiments were drawn from the Jatt (farmer) class from the Malwa, Majha and Doaba regions of the Punjab, which lay on either side of the Sutlej River[45]. As noted, this was for no other reason than the physical characteristics they possessed as farm labourers[46], and with a basic level of education (if any at all) these recruits made the best soldiers because they followed orders and were easy to command.

Colonel Jim Cooke and Captain H.R. Holmes worked on raising the 36th, the latter being the biggest and most powerful man of his time in the Indian Army. It is said that when recruiting for the regiment in Ludhiana, he used to challenge all and any to wrestle him, the condition being that the competitors should enlist if beaten[47]. Sikhs being fine sportsmen and encouraged to take up a challenge flocked to try and beat Holmes. This novel method so stimulated the recruiting that by 1st January 1888 the regiment had been brought to strength of 912 Indian ranks[48]; and the soldiers appeared before the Commander-in-Chief at an exercise camp at Meerut during that winter.

The 36th Sikhs were first dispatched to Delhi in March 1891 but shortly after arriving there they were sent to the district of Manipur to deal with disturbances, where they stayed until November of that year. Returning to Delhi thereafter, orders were issued for the destruction of the old barracks and the creation of new ones, which the regiment undertook and completed in May 1893[49].

In June 1894, Lieutenant Colonel John Haughton took over as commandant of the 36th Sikhs with Major Charles Hamilton Des Voeux as his second-in-command (or 2IC).

Haughton was the son of a hero of the 2nd Afghan War, John Colpoys Haughton. He was born on 22nd August 1852 at Chhota Nagpur and was raised in India. At the age of 13 he was sent to England to attend Uppingham School, a school of high repute. He was educated to go into the Army and aged 17 he passed the exam for Royal Military Academy Sandhurst. He went on to develop at the academy and passed out in 1871, being gazetted an ensign with the 1st Battalion 24th Foot (later the South Wales Borderers). Haughton set out to India from the docks at Liverpool the following January. He was transferred to the 72nd Highlanders who were then quartered in Peshawar, thus began his life time of service on the frontier.

His old form-master, Mr Candler, wrote a tribute to Haughton after his death 'In Memoriam' in the school's magazine, published in June 1898, which gave some brief reminisces of the officer. "He was (as a schoolboy) quiet, gentlemanly and of good report and a very pleasant fellow to deal with", then adding that upon a later meeting after he had become an Indian officer that he appeared "strong and valiant a man to be depended on and trusted."

Haughton joined the 35th Sikhs in May 1887 and assisted them as they were raised. The Indian Army List of January 1897 shows he held the rank of Major when he was first assigned to the 36th but the temporary position of Lt Col was given as befitting the commanding officer of a regiment[50], although he duly attained the rank in full by the next list.

Des Voeux was born in December 1853 in Ireland. He was commissioned as a 2nd Lieutenant with the 37th Foot in 1872 and transferred to the Indian Army in 1884. But shortly thereafter, he embarked for Australia which was at the time going through a turbulent time due to local disturbances. He served as Deputy Assistant Adjutant General and as an Infantry Staff Instructor with the Queensland Defence Forces. He rose to the rank of Major and eight years later in 1892 he finally made his way back to India to join up with the newly formed 36th Sikhs.

In April 1895, the 36th led by its new commander and 2IC was ordered to march to the North West Frontier and Peshawar where it remained until December 1896. In saying farewell to the 36th Sikhs as it embarked on its intended area of operation, Brigadier General E.R Elles CD published a farewell stating that: *"I am well pleased with the regiment in every respect. As long as we have regiments like this in the Native Army we need never be afraid of anything. I hope they may soon have a chance of Active Service and I wish them every luck wherever they may go.[51]"*

Shortly after arriving at Kohat on 31 December 1896 the regiment was ordered to occupy posts on the Samana ridge. The 36th was divided into two parts, Regimental Headquarters and the Right Wing under Lt Col John Haughton occupied Fort Lockhart on 2 January 1897, with detachments at Dar, Sangar, Sartop, Crag, Saragarhi and Fort Gulistan spread over a distance of about five miles. The Left Wing under Capt. W.D Gordon arrived at Parchinar on 8 January with detachments at Thal and Sadda[52].

The twenty-one Sikh soldiers who would find themselves at Saragarhi would have been posted as and when their need arose at the outpost. As the most senior native officer, the equivalent of a sergeant, Havildar Ishar Singh (regimental number 165) would have been assigned the task of manning Saragarhi with a Naik (corporal) under his command. What we know of Ishar Singh's background is that he was born in the village of Jagroan near Ludhiana, and was in his last 30's when he was sent to the Samana. He was a married man but had no children[53].

The sepoys (privates) who made up the fighting force at Saragarhi consisted mainly of young men barely out of their teens such as Gurmukh Singh (regimental number 1733), a 19 year old from the village of Damunda near Jullundur. But there were some who were older and had families at home, such as 23 year old Nand Singh (regimental number 1221) from Attowal near Hoshiarpur who was engaged to be married; and Hira Singh (regimental number 359) from a village near Lahore (in modern day Pakistan) who had a three-month old daughter.

The Sikhs were now in place to play their intended role in checking Pathan aggression in the region and protect India from invasion; they would in the process cement the reputation of their race as the bravest and most loyal of British Indian soldiers.

The Uprising

The Miranzai frontier force had captured the Samana range in 1891 and raised to the ground many of the villages that had once stood there but were destroyed during the conflict. In their place were constructed the forts of Gulistan and Lockhart on the highest ground and various other smaller posts nearby. Roads were created between them to ensure swift troop movement.

This "forward policy" of occupying and controlling enemy ground was further developed in 1892 when the neighbouring Kurram Valley too was placed in British hands[54]. The range overlooked Tirah from the south so eleven posts were placed on it and garrisoned in 1893, with latter posts established at Miranshah, Malakand and Chitral.

These fortified positions enabled closer control to be exercised over the Pathan tribes near British territory, to prevent armed raids into settled districts of India and in certain cases, to guard against Russian movements into the region[55].

But the action of drawing boundaries on the frontier and setting up defensive posts raised fears amongst the tribes that their land and independence was under threat[56]. The Afridis, feeling safe behind the *purdah,* or veil, of the mountains that surrounded their homeland in Tirah, demanded that Britain withdraw from the Samana and Swat Valley altogether[57]. The faithful peace they had kept with the British for sixteen years was broken early in 1897 when they sacked and destroyed five forts close to the Khyber.

This was followed by the siege of Malakand in July, where the British were faced with a force of tribesmen whose lands had been cut by the boundaries created between India and Afghanistan (the Durrand line). It was during this conflict that a twenty-two year old 2nd Lieutenant named Winston Churchill volunteered to serve and fought alongside Sikh units.

At the end of August 1897, the Mullah of Hadda called for a *"lashkar to go out for a holy war and defend the religion of the Holy Prophet.*[58]*"* Later he wrote to all the elders of the Afridi and Orakzai stating: *"The Kafirs have taken possession of all Mussulman [sic] countries and, owing to the lack of spirit on the part of the people, are conquering every region. They have now reached these countries..."* and later that *"I inform you also that you may try your best to further the cause of "jehad" [sic] which is the best of all devotions and the truest of all submissions, so that we may not be ashamed before God on the day of judgement and be glorious before His Prophet.* [59]*"*

The Afridi tribes in turn wrote to the Amir of Afghanistan saying they were helpless in having to take up jihad. The Amir *"turned a deaf ear"* and refused to later listen to their deputation sent to him, replying in a letter: *"what you have done with your own hands you must now carry on your backs. I have nothing to do with you."*

With their holy war against the British now in motion, the Afridi clans were on a collision course with the Indian Army on the Samana and Khyber region. The neighbouring Orakzai clan were persuaded to join the cause and also rose in revolt. At full strength both could muster forty to fifty-thousand fighting men[60].

The scene was now set for a showdown on the Samana ridge between the Pathans and the 36th Sikh regiment led by Lt Col. John Haughton. During the course of September 1897 many heroic deeds were on display, but the self-sacrifice of a handful of staunch soldiers against overwhelming odds would rouse the spirits of all men of valour.

Setting The Scene

With the uprising of the Afridi and Orakzai tribes, Sikh soldiers manned the Samana ridge to defend British interests in India. Lt Col John Haughton's diary from the time gives insight into the events leading up to the attack on Saragarhi[61]:

On the 25th August 1897 information was received that a large force of Orakzai was assembling at Karappa near the tri-junction of the Chagru, Sampagha and Khanki valleys. The intelligence estimated that the fighting strength of the Pathans was approximated 25,000 men but this was later drawn down to 12,000 men.

Haughton was advised by the chief military and political authority not to attack the force; as a consequence two of the minor Samana posts suffered attacks before help could be sent from Hangu.

On the 27th August the enemy was active all along the Samana, attacking on the eastern end the police posts at Lakka and Saifaldara[62] which were captured and destroyed. The latter were garrisoned with tribal levies and there doesn't appear to be any evidence that they stayed to fight their kinsmen.

The enemy force then appeared on the Samana Suk about a mile west of Fort Gulistan, which was held by Major Des Voeux and 150 rifles. This information reached Haughton at Fort Lockhart at around 6.30am who left to aid Gulistan with two British officers and 134 rifles[63].

Des Vouex carried out a reconnaissance of the enemy with sixty men and found them fixed around their position with 4,000 tribesmen. When Haughton arrived to take charge at around 9am he saw that they were outnumbered so withdrew all the troops to inside fort Gulistan[64].

The Orakzai occupied the high ground half a mile west of the fort and opened fire with largely speculative shooting. This became *"very annoying to the troops"* and so Haughton ordered Lieutenant Munn and

Lieutenant Blair with thirty rifles to occupy a picquet 350 yards west of the fort to try and flank the enemy. It was during this mission that Lt Blair was dangerously wounded[65].

In the evening, the Pathans attacked the eastern edge of the range so Haughton sent back to Lockhart half the detachment (or sixty rifles) he had brought earlier.

The next day on the 28th, Haughton too returned to Lockhart to learn that forts at Gogra and Tsalai had been destroyed by the enemy – again the border police made no attempt to defend any of these posts but abandoned them. The Orakzai and Afridi forces continued to swarm on and around the Samana range looking for weak spots, but no further attacks were made. Haughton noted that they wasted their time and opportunities in petty acts of destruction or outrage or in mere sniping by day and night.

On the 30th it was reported that the enemy intended to attack Dhar which was held by border police whose loyalty was somewhat doubtful. Haughton sent as reinforcement a native officer and thirty-seven men of the 36th Sikhs[66].

Days later on the 3rd September 1897 a large force of enemy was observed advancing against Gulistan from the Samana Suk. Haughton galloped to the fort with a small reinforcement, of which he left fifteen rifles along the way at Saragarhi to aid those already there.

Haughton was fired upon on the way – but at Gulistan he found the enemy had planted five standards at Picquet Hill and three within 150 yards of the fort on the south. The enemy crept up and set fire to outbuildings near the fort as well as thorn hedges that were placed as an obstacle in case of any rush to the fort[67]. Twice the fire had to be put out by volunteers from the garrison; six including Sunder Singh and Harnam Singh did so despite heavy enemy gunfire in broad daylight.

Having done so once, they found the fire burning in another place and again the men gallantly sallied forward to put it out there. But in doing so four of the men were wounded[68].

At night and in another act of bravery, Wariam Singh and Gulab Singh volunteered to light a wooden pile outside the fort to light up the area so enemy movements could be seen. They did so in the midst of the Pathans without being hit by enemy bullets.

The enemy withdrew from the firing range at day break on the 4th September after suffering heavy losses. Haughton, thinking the danger was over, returned with his detachment to Lockhart. It was an age-old Pathan tactic to retreat and then re-engage, and upon seeing the British movement the Orakzai returned to Gulistan and kept up their heavy fire at night

This happened again the following day, but the Orakzai were now discouraged by a lack of success. Their *jirgah* tribal council met and decided that unless their neighbours the Afridi supported them on the Samana they would not renew their attacks. Unbeknown to the Orakzai at the time, the Afridi had already met at a *jirgah* days before and decided to send a strong force to oust the British from the Samana forts.

Lockhart and Gulistan were by now on half rations – so General Yeatman-Biggs assembled a force of 2,500 men at Hangu to carry supplies to the forts. The Kurram-Kohat Field Force arrived on the 8th September and immediately sent sappers and miners to fix the parts of Gulistan that had been dug up and damaged during the previous ten days.

Another reconnaissance patrol was sent out to the Samana Suk on the 9th September and found that a strong force of Orakzai and Afridi were assembled near Khangarbur at the junction of the Sampagha and

Khanki valleys, twenty-nine standards were counted giving an indication of enemy numbers. The next day more Afridi arrived, pushing estimates of the gathered tribesmen to between 20,000 to 25,000.

With repairs at Gulistan complete and the troops rations replenished, General Yeatman-Biggs marched his force eastward along the crest of the Samana on 11th September. There he fought a rear-guard action to check the enemy which was intending on the Kohat-Hangu road, but with their own supplies running out his force returned to Hangu. The Orakzai and Afridi immediately doubled back to the Samana forts to lay siege to the area once again.

Sangar was the first to be attacked on the 11th but the forty-four Sikh troops and native officer stationed there were reinforced by thirty-seven men sent by Haughton and the picquet was able to repel that and subsequent attacks[69].

The enemy force was next seen on manoeuvres on the 12th September, near Gogra in the east and the Samana Suk in the west where their numbers were estimated to be from 12,000 to 20,000.

The British had the 36th Sikhs spread along the picquet's and forts, 168 soldiers were at Lockhart under Haughton and Munn while 175 were at Gulistan under Des Voeux. Dhar contained thirty-seven and Sartop and Saragarhi both contained twenty-one Sikhs.

The enemy descended on the Samana and surrounded Saragarhi knowing full well that this would cut communications and troop movements between forts Gulistan and Lockhart, and that with the British spread out it would no longer be possible for Haughton to sent aid. The game of cat and mouse being played out had now reached a climax; the scene was set for a showdown between the Sikhs and the thousands of Pathans encircling Saragarhi.

Above: Lt Col Haughton seated centre surrounded by other regimental officers
Below: Major Des Voeux seated centre with officers and Subedars at Gulistan

Above: the 36th Sikhs at Gulistan with three captured enemy standards
Below: Mrs Des Voeux her children and nanny during the siege at Gulistan

Both photos show fort Gulistan and its hilly surroundings from different angles, above from the east offering a similar view from Saragarhi.

Both photos show fort Lockhart, above from the east and below the horn works built for its defence. The white tents show where the Sikh soldiers slept.

Ruins of Saragarhi after the battle, (previous page) Sikh soldiers on its walls

Sikh soldiers within the burnt out post days after the battle.
Below the cairn built from the ruins bricks.

A Pathan who allegedly fought at Saragarhi stands next to the cairn built by Sikhs soldiers in honour of their dead brethren. The tablet details their heroics.

Right: the memorial obelisk built at fort Lockhart in November 1901, and the tablet listing the names of those who died at Saragarhi.

THE GOVERNMENT OF INDIA
HAVE CAUSED THIS TABLET TO BE ERECTED TO THE MEMORY
OF THE TWENTY ONE NON—COMMISSIONED OFFICERS AND
MEN OF THE 36™ SIKH REGIMENT OF BENGAL INFANTRY,
WHOSE NAMES ARE ENGRAVED BELOW, AS A PERPETUAL
RECORD OF THE HEROISM SHOWN BY THESE GALLANT
SOLDIERS WHO DIED AT THEIR POSTS IN DEFENCE OF THE FORT
OF SARAGARHI, ON THE 12™ SEPTEMBER 1897, FIGHTING AGAINST
OVERWHELMING NUMBERS, THUS PROVING THEIR LOYALTY
AND DEVOTION TO THEIR SOVEREIGN, THE QUEEN EMPRESS OF
INDIA, AND GLORIOUSLY MAINTAINING THE REPUTATION OF THE
SIKHS FOR UNFLINCHING COURAGE ON THE FIELD OF BATTLE.

165 HAVILDAR ISHAR SINGH

332	NAIK	LAL SINGH	834 SEPOY	NARAYAN SINGH
546	L-NAIK	CHANDA SINGH	814	GURMUKH SINGH
1321	SEPOY	SUNDAR SINGH	871	JIVAN SINGH
287		RAM SINGH	1733	GURMUKH SINGH
492		UTTAR SINGH	163	RAM SINGH
182		SAHIB SINGH	1257	BHAGWAN SINGH
359		HIRA SINGH	1265	BHAGWAN SINGH
607		DAYA SINGH	1556	BUTA SINGH
760		JIVAN SINGH	1651	JIVAN SINGH
791		BHOLA SINGH	1221	NAND SINGH

The Last Stand

Saragarhi was manned by twenty-one fighting men, led by Havildar Ishar Singh. Trapped in the midst of 10,000 of the enemy, it meant each individual soldier stood to fight against 476 Pathans. But there was also, within their ranks, a camp follower named Dadh[70]. This individual poses a bit of a mystery, as he first comes to our attention in the reports of the political agent at Hangu who mentions that there was such a non-combatant present. We do not know much more about Dadh, or if indeed this was his name, but he is likely to have been a non-Sikh – possibly a locally recruited Muslim – who was hired specifically to do the menial tasks such as cooking for the troops.

The weapons the men carried, the Martini-Henry, was a breech loading rifle weighing around ten pounds which could be fitted with a 20-inch bayonet for close-quarter combat. It was the most efficient rifle of the time[71]; robust, accurate and simple to use[72] and had earned a reputation as such at Rorke's Drift during the Zulu war of 1879.

To shoot the soldier would open the breech by pushing down on a lever near the trigger, load a round, and raise the lever which would cock the firing mechanism. In the hands of an experienced operator, and with favourable conditions, it was capable of firing 20 rounds per minute. To compare this to a modern weapon, an AK-47 is capable of practically firing 40 rounds per minute on a semi-automatic setting.

At close range to the enemy and from a fixed position with good cover, this gave the Sikhs at Saragarhi an advantage in their defence. But Havildar Ishar Singh would know full well that constant firing would overheat the rifle and cause the cartridges to jam. But he faced a bigger problem - the post only had 400 rounds of ammunition to a man, meaning the Sikhs could not rely on firepower alone to thwart the enemy. The Sikhs could hope to inflict such damage as to demoralise the Pathans from attacking.

The official report states that *"it is no exaggeration to say that there were many thousands of the tribes there collected.*[73]*"* They swarmed around the three sides of Saragarhi (the fourth side was faced the cliff drop) while thousands more vigorously attacked Gulistan; a third body was positioned at the villages on the route to Lockhart so aid could not be sent from there.

As the reality of the situation dawned upon the Sikhs, fleeing or asking for safe sanctuary would not have been considered an option, their martial creed called for them to take a stand. Nor could the words of the wily Pathans, who offered safe passage, be trusted as they had broken many an oath against the British already. The enemy were fixed on a lust for *jihad* but the Sikhs they met were firm in living up their name as lions and embracing the battle in the spirit of their faith and forefathers.

With an entrenched position the Sikhs could hope to hold out for as long as possible until reinforcements could distract or push the enemy away. Havildar Ishar Singh knew full well that their commander, Lieutenant Colonel Haughton, was not one to leave a single soldier behind let alone allow the strategic communications post to be threatened; help was expected as were reinforcement from Hangu.

Each soldier had a duty to perform in defending Saragarhi, from Ishar Singh who was leading his men and reminding them of their Sikh virtue, to Gurmukh Singh who was positioned in the tower to continue sending heliograph signals, to the sepoys who positioned themselves in their firing positions. It was not expected that Dadh would fight, but with the instinct for survival kicking in it is probable that he assisted in the defence by providing the troops with water, rations and helping any injured.

The Havildar rallied his men to fight in the name of their Guru and with the words of Guru Gobind Singh from their national anthem ringing in their ears: to fix their mind on God, to be righteous and not be intimidated by their enemies. The creed of the Sikhs meant they were fully aware of the glory that awaited them should they die on the battlefield, so they prepared themselves for the ultimate sacrifice but with hopes that they would live to fight another day.

The best indication of what happened next come from the observations of those at forts Lockhart and Gulistan, which was in line of sight of the siege. At about 9am the Pathans began their attack by rushing Saragarhi in hopes of overcoming the walls but were repulsed with losses, at least 60 killed and wounded[74]. The enemy resorted to taking shelter behind the rocks, folds and dips in the ground so as to work their way under cover close up to the walls of the post while continuing to fire on the garrison. Using the ground in this way was a cautious practice for the Pathans who were otherwise exposed.

But during this first attack two Pathans stayed behind at the post, being *"fully cognisant of the defects in the flank defence"* of the post and its construction they *"remained close under the walls of the north-west bastion where there was a dead angle[75]."* They were not seen by the Sikhs inside Saragarhi, possibly covered from view and fire. These two began digging under the tower while Ishar Singh and his men were focused on the large mass of Pathans trying to get through the door of the post. This was clearly seen by Major Des Voeux at Gulistan, who tried in vain to warn the garrison by heliograph signal of what was happening. He was unable to do so, possibly as the Pathans had set fire to bushes in the vicinity to create a smokescreen.

Gurmukh Singh was sending messages of what was happening to Lt Col Haughton at Lockhart. At about noon, the signaller flashed back to the commander that one sepoy had been killed and one was wounded. Three rifles had been broken by the enemies' bullets[76]. Haughton cautioned the garrison at Saragarhi several times not to waste their ammunition, but to keep the enemy at bay while reinforcements were mustered.

Haughton then sent Lt Munn with fourteen soldiers of the Royal Irish Regiment (who'd been left behind sick from earlier by General

Yeatman-Biggs). Armed with Lee-Metford rifles their task was to create a diversion a short distance away by long-range volleys in hopes that the Pathans would disengage from Saragarhi, but this had no effect on the enemy who saw the superiority of their position.

For the next three hours at Saragarhi, the defenders were kept under a heavy fire, at a few yards range, if they showed themselves by the tribesmen shooting their jezail's. With this cover, vigorous assaults were made by the Pathans to set the doorway of the post on fire[77]; the post's weak point being a wooden door rather than a metal one. Indeed the officers and soldiers were aware of this soft spot; one young British officer with the Royal Engineers who was on the Samana at the time wrote that the doors of all the smaller forts were not iron-plated and that to give the impression that they were bullet-proof and fire-proof they had been covering them with kerosene tins.[78].

The enemy tried in vain with several advances to try and gain the upper hand in the siege, but the Sikhs inside kept them at bay with their rifle fire. But what Ishar Singh and his sepoys could not see though were the two Pathans located close by on the other side of the wall who continued their digging.

Hours later at 3pm, Haughton received a signal that ammunition was running out at Saragarhi. Despite not knowing about the diggers at the site, the commander was at once determined to make a final attempt to relieve the garrison, leaving two officers and 78 men behind at Lockhart, and with Lt Munn and 93 rifles in tow he advanced cautiously towards Saragarhi. But the Pathans almost immediately threatened his right flank and could only be checked by gunfire from Lockhart and by a flanking party detached to cover Haughton's right. The commander moved cautiously to aide his men but he only got around a hundred yards when it was too late.

Just after 3pm, Major Des Vouex saw that the wall at the dead angle where the diggers were working began to fall in leaving a large breach; the hole that was forming was clearly visible to the naked eye from

Gulistan. The two Pathan diggers who had stayed behind in the initial rush to the post now began to beat down the stones with sticks and moments later the wall fell down in great heaps leaving a gap of around seven feet broad and twelve feet high[79].

Forty minutes later and with a final cry to advance the enemy rushed the breach while at the same time made for unhinged door, which had been shattered by rifle fire. Ishar Singh and his men ran down from their positions on the wall to defend the hole as the enemy swarmed through the gap that had been made. As the tribesmen crowded over their own dead and injured to get into Saragarhi, the few Sikhs that were left inside put up a stubborn defence but had only one option to retreat into the inner defences. Ishar Singh is believed to have covered his men and fought on in hand-to-hand combat before being killed.

Another sepoy who had secured the guard room door from the inside and used his rifle to fight on was burnt to death as the Pathans set the post on fire - his foes admitted later that he accounted for twenty of their dead before his end came.

In another part of the post signaller Gurmukh Singh heliographed back to Gulistan stating: *"they are getting in now; shall I go on signalling or shall I take a rifle?*[80]" As the last of the soldiers left he had seen all twenty of his comrade's fight to the bitter end. With the encroaching enemy surrounding him, Gurmukh Singh fired on until he got to the last round of ammunition. Knowing his end was nigh he let out a loud battle cry, or *jaikara*, and shot himself so as not to fall prisoner to the enemy[81].

Having slain the entire garrison, including the camp follower Dadh, and thrown down the walls the enemy now quickly moved to set fire to the rest of the ruins. A loud explosion was heard by Haughton, probably due (according to the official report) to the blowing up of a large number of cartridges which the enemy in their hour of success had failed to discover[82].

Saragarhi had fallen and the twenty-one Sikhs inside had fought to the bitter end despite such heavy numbers against them. But the enemy paid a price for their victory, 180 to 200 Pathans were killed, and the battle on the Samana was far from over.

Gallantry At Gulistan

Saragarhi had fallen by 4pm, at which time the Pathans, encouraged by their success, turned to attack Gulistan which now could not communicate with Lockhart. At the latter were two British officers alongside 168 native soldiers from the 36th Sikhs, who would be helpless in aiding their comrades.

At Gulistan, Major Des Voeux manned the defences with three other officers and 175 Sikhs. They would remain in their positions without rest or relief for more than fifty hours. They neither had time for food nor comfort as the enemy were constantly on them. Worse still, Mrs Des Voeux was also besieged with other women and her children. The official record also notes that the two cooks of the post were cut off from returning to the post after going out for firewood, were captured and killed by the enemy.

By night, the Pathans kept up a steady fire on the fort – and at dawn on the 13th September the enemy was found to have crept up within twenty yards of the walls, taking advantage of every bank and fold on the ground. They built up shelters for themselves from the stone and rock and had planted their standards on this line of makeshift sangars (or small temporary fortified positions).

Major Des Voeux recognised that the enemy could deliver a similar blow as at Saragarhi to Gulistan because the construction of the fort had the same defect – the dead ground immediately at the point of each bastion[83]. And so Des Voeux set about clearing the lower rooms in the bastions and with the bags containing rations built up breastworks across the weak corners. In each bastion was a sentry to listen for any noise of hammering, and ten men placed to defend it[84].

With the enemy putting sangars up within yards of the fort, it was all too apparent that they planned to breach the walls as at Saragarhi. And so Major Des Vouex decided to send out a sortie of Sikhs against these.

A Pathan standard was picked out twenty yards away from the south-western end of the horn works and fixed as the point of attack.

Havildar Kala Singh volunteered with his section of sixteen Sikhs for the attack. At 8am a heavy fire was opened from the fort on the Pathans, while Kala Singh and his men slipped out of the southern gate. They crept along the face of the fort to the south-west corner and then with bayonets fixed charged the sangar. Despite the element of surprise the Sikhs got to within six paces of the enemy before the Pathans returned fire. The enemy now displayed three standards at the site, meaning there were more of them, and the Sikhs dropped to the ground for cover and began firing at their positions.

Instantly and without orders, Havildar Sunder Singh and eleven other Sikhs on their own accord leapt over the walls of Gulistan to the support of their comrades. Picking and carrying the first attack party along, they charged the designated sangar, driving out the Pathans and capturing the three standards. Amid the ringing cheers and war cries of their fellow Sikhs the men rescaled the walls to safety.

But two wounded men were found to be missing. This time Sepoy Bela Singh jumped over the wall to find them, and was joined by two others. Before the Pathans could recover from their surprise and alarm, the Sikhs had brought in the missing men who were gravely wounded.

Thirteen of the 29 men involved in the attack were severely wounded, two gravely. But the effect produced well repaid the loss and is considered the turning point in the fight – putting heart into the defenders and dealing a blow to the enemy who despite their overwhelming numbers had lost three standards. Every wounded man fit to stand and shoot returned to his duty as soon as his wound had been dressed, some did not even report their injuries.

There was a nursemaid at hand to attend to the wounded, but the reason why Theresa McGrath found herself under siege at Gulistan was instead because of the pregnant wife of Major Des Voeux who'd been at her husband's side at the fort. Mrs Des Voeux went into labour while the fort was under fire, and gave birth to a baby girl, who was named Violet Samana.

Before dark, field guns were observed from Gulistan firing in the Miranzai valley. A message from General Yeatman-Biggs stated that his force would relieve the garrison the next day. The Orakzai and Afridis, estimated to be numbering up to twelve thousand, surrounded Gulistan at dawn on the 14th September. Up to 8,000 of the enemy were observed holding a strong position on the Saragarhi heights while several thousand others were on the Samana Suk.

A couple of hours later, at 9am, British field guns began firing from the Miranzai valley onto the hills west of Gulistan. Soon after shells began bursting over the heights near Saragarhi as General Yeatman-Biggs and the Kurram-Kohat Field Force edged forward. The enemy there suffered heavy losses and quickly abandoned the heights[85]. By 10am the relieving force had arrived at Lockhart, Haughton and his men now joined the General in relieving Gulistan.

Feeling no further need to spare his ammunition, Major Des Voeux ordered his troops to open fire upon the enemy with every available rifle. The 2nd Punjab Infantry and Haughton's 36th Sikhs too hurried to attack the thousands of Pathans gathered around Gulistan, but were given no chance to close with the enemy as the tribesmen retreated down the hill away from the fort with rifle fire from the troops there whizzing past them. By 1pm the relieving force had reached Gulistan and the siege was over.

One such English soldier in the relief force was J.A Lindsay who arrived at Saragarhi after the bloody battle to find the location littered with the bodies of the enemy, some had been killed by the Sikhs while others had been shelled by the relieving force.

The Sikhs inside Saragarhi had perished in the flames and a cairn would be built from the rubble of the post to mark their final resting place. Lindsay wrote home describing the difficulty of getting to the ridge and the horrors of the scene there: *"Saragarhi is an awful sight that is the face which 21 Sikhs behaved so admirably... the place is anything but sanitary as of course not much burying could be done."* Lindsay goes on to pay tribute to the soldiers, adding: *"The detachment of the 36th Sikhs marched over from Gulistan this morning carrying the standards they had captured from the enemy – they are a splendid corps and have made a great name for themselves.*[86]*"*

It was officially estimated that the Orakzai and Afridi casualties numbered 400 killed and 600 seriously wounded in the attacks on the Samana forts. The *lashkars* which had gathered wilted away and posed no further threat in the area.

On the British side, there were twenty-one Sikh casualties at Saragarhi plus the camp follower Dadh. At Gulistan the conflict claimed the lives of two Sikh soldiers and thirty-nine were wounded. Lt Blair was dangerously injured while Havildar Kala Singh, who led the attack against the Pathan sangar, succumbed to his wounds.

Aftermath And Tirah

In the immediate aftermath of the actions on the Samana, the Kurram-Kohat Field Force under General Yeatman-Biggs remained to repair roads, the posts and the telegraph line. A *jirga* of the tribes was interviewed by him on the 17th September; they were submissive and accepted the previous conditions placed before them[87].

But the events on the Samana had given impetus to the British mission to subdue the Afridi and Orakzai tribes once and for all. The tribes recognised that preparations were indeed being made for the invasion of their country. The force under Yeatman-Biggs was, on the 3rd October, incorporated into the Tirah Expeditionary Force which was launched under the command of General Sir William Lockhart.

On the 6th October the General issued a proclamation to the tribes that had caused such havoc on the range, referring to the treaty of 1881 that saw allowances paid for the maintenance of order and abstinence of outrages in British territory. *"These observations have been on the whole faithfully observed"* he remarked but added that the tribes had since broken their engagements, attacked, plundered and burnt the posts in the Khyber[88].

For this action all tribal allowances for the safe upkeep of the area were declared forfeit and a force despatched under Lockhart's command to *"announce from the heart of their country the final terms of the British Government[89]."* More than 34,000 British and Indian troops marched to subdue the Pathans who had risen up in revolt.

Lockhart added that the British *"had never the intention nor wish to inflict unnecessary damage on the tribes, provided they immediately make submission and reparation."* The terms would be announced to the jirgas of the tribes in Tirah[90]. But first the British had to fight their way there; the Pathans had no sense of surrender.

The 36th Sikhs played a crucial role in the mission as it joined the 4th Brigade of the Tirah Expeditionary Force, initially protecting the right flank of the brigade on the Samana Suk as it moved to its objective. The inaction though was hard to bear for Lt Col Haughton and his Sikhs who wanted to avenge the butchery of Saragarhi[91]. But there would be opportunity enough for the regiment to see action.

The expedition began with the capture of the Dargai heights on the 18th October; and then their subsequent loss due to the hot conditions and for want of water. It was recaptured two days later at the cost of 199 soldiers. On the 29th October, the regiment shared in the attack on the Sampagha Pass, and the next day on the Arhanga Pass[92]. The expedition would continue through difficult terrain and test the British in a mountainous area they had yet to venture, the Tirah homeland.

Dragging into November the expedition wound its way through enemy territory, villages including Saran Sar (on the 9th) were destroyed. The Pathans deployed their stubborn tactics of engaging and retreating and knowing the terrain better than the British waged a guerrilla war on them. The 36thSikhs encamped in the Maidan Valley until 12th November taking part in daily foraging expeditions for food. On the 13th the regiment formed the advance guard to the 3rd Brigade and was left on the heights of Kotal at the Tseri Kandao to hold the pass[93].

While the 36th were posted on the heights, another Sikh regiment showed bravery and valour on the 16th November. The 15th Sikhs had many wounded and being only sixty in number barely held the southern edge of a pine wood near the Saran Sar. They were rushed by a hundred or more Pathans, who got to around ten yards of the Sikhs but were fought off. Not many of the enemy survived[94].

The 36th Sikhs continued along with the expedition through December and January 1898 until the tragic death of Lt Col Haughton, an officer who could always be found at the fore leading his men. The commander was tasked to be the advance guard as the British made their way up the Shinkamar pass. Two companies, or two-hundred men, of the 36th Sikhs went to scale the heights while Haughton led the central attack. Haughton was ordered to reconnoitre caves beyond the pass and led his men forward, but a flanking company which was to protect his rear from the heights misunderstood the order and also followed, in the process exposing the rear.

With this the Pathans seized their chance and scaled the heights. Having completed the reconnaissance, Haughton retired down the Kotal but was cut off from the body of his men. With the Pathans trapping him, the commander took up a rifle and with the few men with him made a defiant last stand, much in the way his men had done at Saragarhi. Two Sikhs were killed in the ensuing fire fight and Haughton told the remaining soldiers to fix bayonets and fire the last of their ammunition. But the order to charge the enemy never came; Haughton was hit with a sniper bullet to the head.

With their commander's death, the expedition into the Tirah homeland was now at an end for the 36th Sikhs who had paid a terrible price for the defence of the Samana and subsequent actions against the tribes who had destroyed Saragarhi. In total the regiment lost two British officers in Tirah plus seven wounded, fifteen Sikhs killed and 57 wounded.

Haughton was buried in Peshawar, at the Tehkal Cemetery (or Gora Qabristan). The memorial placed at his grave was ornate, a large marble cross resting on another three pieces of marble containing inscriptions in his memory. On our recent research trip to the location we rediscovered the site, but what was left was simply (and perhaps thankfully) the stone that contained his name and description.

Haughton's fellow officers at the time raised funds to commission a memorial plaque in his honour, which was placed at the chapel of Uppingham School, Rutland in 1899. The plaque carried the simple inscription: *"Sacred to the memory of Lt. Col. John Haughton, Commandant 36th Sikhs, who was killed in action at the Shin Kamar Pass NW Frontier of India, 29th January 1898 while boldly defending a* *position to the last against overwhelming odds. This brass is erected by his brother officers of the 35th and 36th Sikhs."*

The regiment undertook no further expeditions after Tirah; in 1900 the 36th Sikhs was detailed for escort duty in connection with the Chitral Reliefs and in 1901 moved to Malakand. In January 1904 the regiment moved to Peshawar, while the next year in November it took part in a review by the Prince of Wales in Rawalpindi[95].

The courageous last stand at Saragarhi would provide the most memorable part of the regiment's sacrifice, one which would do the 36th Sikhs and its subsequent incarnations proud. But the actions of the 36th Sikhs as a whole during their time on the frontier are also worthy of admiration and everlasting memory.

Recognition And Reward

The 36[96]th Sikhs were lavishly rewarded for their bravery and heroics on the Samana, thirty-three soldiers received the Indian Order of Merit[96] including two Sepoys and a Havildar who died of their wounds. The twenty-one Sikhs at Saragarhi would also receive the distinction posthumously as their heroic action was quickly recognised by the British and reported on in newspapers back in Britain(see Appendix B).

Despatches from the late Major-General Yeatman-Biggs were sent to the Commander-in-Chief, India General Sir George Stuart White VC describing the events on the Samana. These were in turn published in the Times on 12th February 1898 (see Appendix C1). The Generals march to the relief of Gulistan was said to have been: "*performed under very trying circumstances, owing to the heat and to a great scarcity of water en route; but the force successfully accomplished its object with the same gallantry and cheerfulness as have been evinced on every occasion by our troops during the various operations which have recently taken place on the North-West Frontier.*"

Particular attention was drawn to the actions performed by the 36th Sikhs who were at the fore of defending several posts on the Samana. The Commander-in-Chief noted that: "*At Sangar the small garrison made a sortie and gallantly captured a standard from the enemy, while the brilliant defence of Fort Gulistan by the detachment under the command of Major Des Voeux reflects the greatest credit on that officer and the garrison of the post. The Government of India will, His Excellency is assured, appreciate fully the intrepid manner in which the late Havildar Kala Sing (sic)led the sortie from the Gulistan Fort, and also the conduct of Havildar Sundar Singh, who assisted his comrades at a critical moment.*"

Saragarhi was cited in a more sombre tone, due to the deep regret for the loss of the garrison, with the Commander-in-Chief recording his: "*admiration of the heroism shown by those gallant soldiers. Fighting against overwhelming numbers they died at their post, thus proving their loyalty and devotion to their sovereign, while upholding to the last the traditional bravery of the Sikh nation..."*

The Governor-General Victor Bruce, the Earl of Elgin, too expressed his *"admiration of the brilliant defence of Fort Gulistan by the 36th Sikhs, and of the post of Saragarhi"* describing Havildar Ishar Singh as *"displaying a heroic devotion which has never been surpassed in the annals of the Indian Army."* (See Appendix C2)

The news of the events on the frontier were brought to the attention of Queen Victoria at Balmoral Castle, who received a telegram days after the battle on 16th September giving accounts of the fighting and of what she described as the *"splendid behaviour of the Sikhs in defending Fort Cavagnari for 30 hours."*[97]

Recognition on behalf of the Crown of events on the Samana was accorded in July 1898, when Her Majesty's Government recorded their *"high appreciation of the gallant conduct and admirable qualities"* shown by those engaged on the frontier, adding: *"They especially desire to record their admiration of the 36th Sikhs, who were all killed fighting to the last in defence of the post of Saragarhi."* (See Appendix C3)

After the Tirah campaign, Sir William Lockhart had an audience with the Queen at Balmoral on Wednesday 12th October 1898 – a year and a month after the battle of Saragarhi. Her Majesty would no doubt have heard more from the General about the events on the Samana and the bravery of the Sikhs.

Lockhart had himself earlier in January 1898 received a splendid letter, two in fact one in Urdu colourfully printed on paper alongside another in English printed on silk; from leading Sardars of Rawalpindi. In it the prominent Sikhs speak of their *"feelings of admiration at the gallantry displayed by your troops during the recent campaign in Tirah*[98]*."* They go on to invoke Saragarhi and the last stand of its martyrs which *"prove* *by their example that in time of need the Sikhs would die to a man in service of Her Most Gracious Majesty the Queen Empress."* What's remarkable about this address is that written just month after Saragarhi they already speak in an emotive sense of what the battle means to both the British and Sikhs. (See the letter in full in Appendix D).

The actions of Theresa McGrath, who delivered a baby while under siege at Gulistan and helped nurse the wounded, was brought to the attention of Lord Lansdowne, the. Secretary of War with whom lay the recommendation to Her Majesty The Queen for the Royal Red Cross, .a decoration conferred for "special exertions in providing for the nursing, or for attending to, sick and wounded soldiers and sailors[99]."

By 1898 pressure grew for the award to be granted, with The Daily Chronicle even calling for women who showed conspicuous courage and self-sacrifice to receive the Victoria Cross itself. It cited the example of the nurse who "a time when the stoutest man's nerves were shaken, Miss McGrath, by her courage and presence of mind, saved many of the garrison from bleeding to death. As well as enduring all the hardships of the siege, Miss McGrath nursed the dying and wounded night and day with unceasing care and courage, but has received no recognition whatever of her devotion and heroism."[100]

The award of the Royal Red Cross medal was duly granted to Theresa McGrath at Windsor Castle in May 1899 by the Queen who wrote in her diaries, that she had *"behaved most heroically[101]."*

Those who fought on the North West Frontier were recognised by the Secretary of State for India who sanctioned a gratuity for those engaged in the region. Issued at a rate of *"Rs. 24 per share for the British and Rs. 12 for native soldiers"* the amount was paid to the heirs of those killed in action or who died of disease during the operations in 1897.

The Indian Order of Merit (IOM), then the highest medal for gallantry that could be awarded to native soldiers was awarded posthumously to the twenty-one. The IOM was on par with the Victoria Cross, but given in three classes. The Sikhs at Saragarhi received the entry level, third class, while their families were admitted to the wound pension associated with the medal and given an additional allowance which was issued according to the soldiers rank to their descendents.

As well as the IOM, the campaign medal, the India Medal 1985 - 1902 was also awarded for campaigns on the Punjab Frontier and included Samana and Tirah.

The Gulistan Bahadurs, who defended their outpost, were also issued the IOM 3rd class. 34 of their number achieved this accolade and issued the medal, including three that were gravely wounded and honoured in the same manner as the Saragarhi heroes. Another 30 soldiers also received the Indian Distinguished Service Medal. 38 soldiers received Mentioned in Despatches.

Further recognition came from the Viceroy of India, Lord Curzon, who eulogized the Sikh race at an event in Lahore. Having met veterans who'd served the Crown from China to Egypt he told audiences that: *"Never may the day arise when the British Government, in time of need, cannot rely upon his stanch unquestionable service!"*

The Viceroy further added that: *"The Sikh soldiers of the Army of the Queen has given many illustrations of heroic courage in 50 years fighting for the British Raj since the time, now nearly forgotten, which they fought so well against us, so that the name of your race has become almost synonymous in the English language with traditions of desperate courage and unflinching loyalty. There are many qualities required to constitute the ideal soldier – bravery, endurance, a certain aptitude of intellect, discipline – but I am not sure that above them all I would not disregard of self that impels a man to die at his post, as the Sikhs did at Saragarhi, unmurmuring, even happy, in fighting against overwhelming odds."* (See Appendix C4)

The speech on 7th April 1899 came ahead of Vaisakhi commemorations to mark the creation of the Khalsa and as a monument to the bravery of the 36th Sikhs was being planned for Amritsar and through public subscription of the Pioneer newspaper at Ferozepur also: *"These two monuments"* he said *"will testify to later ages at once the valour of your race and the gratitude of mine."*

By November 1901, the Times was reporting on the memorial to the twenty-one Sikhs at Saragarhi which was proposed to be placed at Fort Lockhart and at Amritsar. It read that: *"The Government of India have caused this memorial to be erected to the memory of twenty-one* non-commissioned officers and men of the 36th Sikhs, whose names are engraved below as a perpetual record of the heroism shown by these gallant soldiers who died at their posts in the defence of the frontier post Saragarhi, September 12th 1897, fighting against overwhelming numbers and thus proving their loyalty and devotion to the Sovereign Queen-Empress of India, and gloriously maintaining the reputation of the Sikhs for unflinching courage on the field of battle."* (See Appendix C5)

Further adding below the names of the twenty-one that: *"It will be remembered that in the autumn of 1897, when the Orakzai Afridis rose, they attacked the Saragarhi post on the Samana. Saragarhi fell after a heroic defence, the enemy having mined the tower before the late Gen. Sir Penn Symons could sufficiently reinforce the Samana range."*

The Saragarhi memorial was unveiled in Amritsar on 16th April 1902 by the Commander-in-Chief General Sir Arthur Power Palmer in the presence of the Lieutenant-Governor, officials and representatives of all the Sikh regiments, the Times remarked that *"the ceremony was most impressive."* (See Appendix C6)

Addressing the audience as *"Sirdars and Khalsa Log"* (meaning 'folk' in Punjabi) Power Palmer put forward his personal joy in being at the ceremony, saying that: *"It is particularly pleasing to me individually to have an opportunity of showing by my presence here today my* admiration and affection for the great Sikh nation, as I have been associated with Sikh soldiers from almost my earliest recollections of the Indian army. Belonging as I do to that last dwindling number who were present in this land in the days of the Indian Mutiny, I can remember the relief that it was to us all to find that the Sikhs and the people of the Punjab were staunch when others proved themselves a foe worthy of our steel a little more than ten years previously [during the Anglo-Sikh wars] could be counted on to assist us in our hour of need.[102]"

Moving on to the recognition of the heroics of Saragarhi, the Commander-in-Chief observed that: "The memorial is the outcome of a spontaneous appreciation of the gallantry of a representative detachment of your nation, belonging to the 36th Sikhs, who proved that they still possessed one of the finest of characteristics of a soldier – that they preferred death to surrender.[103]"

The Commander-in-Chief underlined the importance of the memorial at Amritsar and the lessons it had for others in that: "It was felt that this conduct, which was so characteristic of the Sikh nation and its traditions, ought to be kept in remembrance as an example to others of how brave men should behave when facing fearful odds so memorials have been erected at the head-quarters of the Sikh religion and on the site of the old Saragarhi Post in order that as long as British rule in India lasts, the brave Sikh soldiers of the King shall realise that their deeds shall never be forgotten, and that other classes may understand that we know how to appreciate men who fight for us and show by their conduct that they can die for us.[104]"

Power Palmer thereafter gave much recognition to the heroics of the Sikhs at Saragarhi in his comments, but the act of remembrance itself would largely remain an Indian military affair.

Remembrance

The act of remembering those who fought on the Samana was continued by those who fought at the battle and who had served with the Sikhs during Empire, but for future generations it's place in history would be cemented when the day of the battle, 12th September, was soon thereafter declared by the Government of India to be observed as a regimental holiday in perpetuity for all regiments enlisting Sikhs[105].

Saragarhi was further granted as a Battle Honour to the 36th Sikhs and in 1900 an order issued authorising the regiment to bear upon its colours and appointment the honorary distinctions specified in commemoration of its gallant conduct and distinguished services on the Punjab Frontier, Samana and Tirah[106].

Thereafter during the Great War, the 36th Sikhs were involved in China at Tsing Tao in 1914, in Mesopotamia in 1916, at the battle of Hai in 1917 and in Persia in 1918. In all these arenas of war the belief of fighting to the last in accordance with the national anthem of their creed and in the spirit of Saragarhi prevailed.

In 1922 and after the British Indian Army was reformed to a multi-battalion regimental system, the 36th became the 4[th]Battalion of the 11th Sikh Regiment. During the Second World War, the regiment saw action in Egypt, Italian East Africa, Libya, Iraq, Palestine, Lebanon, Syria and Italy[107]. There too the heroics of Saragarhi were remembered when fighting fascism.

After the war, and just days before India and Pakistan became independent, a service notice appeared in the Times which continued the tradition of remembrance. A luncheon was to be held in England for those connected with the 36th Sikhs (4 Battalion Sikh Regiment) on Saragarhi day. (See Appendix C8) Sadly it would be the last notice in the paper, as the regiment of Saragarhi became a foreign entity.

India and Pakistan were granted independence, and the 4th Battalion of the Sikh Regiment went to the sub-continent. The new regiment would go on to see action in Jammu and Kashmir, Sindh and East Pakistan (before it became Bangladesh). But the regiment never forgot Saragarhi, and continued the act of annually remembering the heroics on the Samana by marking the regimental holiday with prayers in all of their units. An *Akhand Path*, or continuous recitation of Sikh scriptures, takes place at Ferozepur and Amritsar to this day.

Auditoriums at various Sikh army training centres have been dedicated to the battle including the Saragarhi Hall at the infantry school at Belgaum, Karnataka. At the regimental centre in Ramgarh, Bihar; a memorial service is held annually with awards given to soldiers who have excelled in the names of Havildar Ishar Singh and the camp follower Dadh.

Prayers also take place in every unit of 4 Sikh, in marking the regimental day in this manner, Sikhs serving in the Indian army continue their remembrance of the event and of those soldiers who fought and died in accordance with their martial creed. On special occasions, such as in 1997 on the 100th anniversary of the battle, parades are held and larger scale commemorations with special guests invited. On the centenary celebration, the battle was depicted with actors dressed up in the uniforms of that era.

The most significant act of remembrance though continues to take place at the memorials to Saragarhi in Amritsar and Ferozepur with pilgrimages and visits from those who either know its heroic story or have some connection to the Sikh regiment involved. Some might even stumble upon it by coincidence. While the memorial obelisk and the cairn at the battle site on the Samana itself have fallen into a state of dilapidation because it has not been properly maintained, the memorials in the Sikh heartland of Punjab give a contrasting picture of how the event is remembered today.

In the holy city of Amritsar the memorial built by the Government of India in 1901 lies in a state of disrepair, it is located just half a mile from the Harimandir Sahib and the board in charge of overseeing places of worship – the SGPC - are building a hostel for tourists and pilgrims which threatens to loom over and dwarf Gurdwara Saragarhi. Nonetheless should one venture there, the memorial provides a hidden gem of solitary reflection upon the men of the 36th Sikhs who died at Saragarhi with their names etched in stone in English and Gurmukhi. A marble panel added in 1997 from the current 4 Sikhs marks the centenary of the battle itself. The history boards placed there also narrate the story of Saragarhi in Hindi and Urdu.

At Ferozepur today, the memorial created through subscriptions to the Pioneer newspaper stands in much better condition, placed at the centre of beautiful kept gardens with regular visitors and *langar*, or free kitchen, serving food. Much more can be said of the memorial and the sight it brings visitors because it is kept in better condition (perhaps as it is near the 4 Sikh regiment cantonment).

Outside the memorial are placed canon at each of the four entrances; one light 6-pound field gun and two 9-pound wheeled carriage guns. The latter is an example of a bronze field gun which saw service in the East India Company during the Anglo-Sikh Wars, rare as these were melted down for scrap metal and replaced by iron and steel artillery pieces from the 1860's. The lighter gun is dated 1856 and from its inscription we can tell it was built by Captain A. Broome who was in charge of the British gun foundry at Cossipore on the Hooghly river near Calcutta. It is possible that these treasured pieces saw action against the Sikhs and during India Mutiny, but now in a twist of irony they stand as guardians to the sacred Sikh scriptures placed inside the Gurdwara[108] - fulfilling a ceremonial purposes in a silent salute to those fallen in countless conflicts.

Inside, plaques on the wall carry the names of the twenty-one Sikhs and their heroics also but eight tablets containing *shabads*, or religious verses, eulogize the significance of the Sikh sacrifice through what it means spiritually to the creed. These were presented by the tenth Raja of Faridkot, HH Balbir Singh Bahadur, in commemoration of the Sikhs of his state who fell at Saragarhi.

One of the *shabad* tablets contains a verse from the *Sarbloh Granth* written by the tenth Guru Gobind Singh which praises the quality of the pure brotherhood he created:

Khalsa is he who shuns back-biting
Khalsa is he who fights foremost
Khalsa is he who respects others rights
Khalsa is he who loves God
Khalsa is he who devotes himself to the Guru
Khalsa is he who confronts arms
Khalsa is he who helps the needy
Khalsa is he who wages war against evil
Khalsa is he who rides well
Khalsa is he who is first in War.

Another *shabad* tablet contains a verse from *Chaubis Avtar* in *Dasam Granth* praising a person who embraces both saintly and soldierly virtues:

Blessed is he in this world who while repeating God's name fights heart and soul.
Who does not regard this mortal frame as everlasting
Who crosses the ocean of this universe in the boat of fame
Who makes his body a palace of courage with wisdom as bright as a lamp
And who removes cowardice from his mind with the sword of knowledge.

These verses give direction to the Sikh martial psyche and an indication of the values espoused by those who fight and died on the Samana. While such guidance from the Guru is invaluable, so too in remembering the actions of those who died in war is establishing the truth of what happened in order to appreciate why they fought.

The story of Saragarhi has become detached from historic fact and accrued its own legend with many myths being created around it. But efforts to bring the Indian service of remembrance of Saragarhi to the western world have in recent years gathered pace, with the 12th September being marked with moments of silence and prayers at Gurdwaras in the United Kingdom in particular. But lacking in the understanding of Saragarhi in this endeavour is the significance the battle still has for British Sikhs and the ways in which it can continue to inform their connection to their country. An endeavour this publication hopes has now been created.

The Legacy

Sikhs stood firm, loyal and did their duty during the conflict in 1897 and in the process earned their spurs on the frontier. This point cannot be overstated, as not only did this cement the relationship of Sikhs as the most trusted of soldiers for the British but it showed that as a martial race they could be trusted to fight above and beyond all others. In this regard a contrast can be made between the Sikhs and the local Pathan levies that did not fight and ran away from their outposts on the frontier during the uprising.

Fate led to the twenty-one Sikhs being placed at the Saragarhi post, they were not special or extra-human but rather ordinary Sikh soldiers who were initiated into the Khalsa. So the saint-soldierly values codified by Guru Gobind Singh – that of courage, honour, selflessness and commitment to their cause – ensured they did their duty and stood firm in the face of overwhelming odds. They continued the legacy of the Guru's martial spirit, themselves taking inspiration from heroic last stands by the Sikhs such as at the battle of Chamkaur, and proving once again that the Khalsa can take on overwhelming odds.

What was extraordinary is that their entire regiment (indeed race) would have done the same as them. Indeed, the psyche of the creed shows this to be a feat that could all too easily be repeated by Sikhs now and in future. This is best demonstrated by Lord Kitchener of Khartoum who cited in a lecture another example of Sikh heroics in 1903, that of: *"a small party of 48 men of the 2nd Sikhs in Somaliland who overwhelmed by superior numbers and having fired away their last cartridge, fell to a man on the ground which they had defended so gallantly throughout the day."* Kitchener decreed that *"Such men – simple in their religion, free in not observing caste prejudice, manly in their warlike creed, and in being true sons of the soil ... but brave, strong and true – are of priceless value to the empire.*[109]*"*

Bravery came as standard for the Sikhs, and we also see during the conflict on the Samana various acts of gallantry at Gulistan and Lockhart. The singular bravery of individuals there, such as Wariam Singh and Gulab Singh who volunteered to light a wooden pile near the enemy to see enemy movements; affirms that Sikhs would fight selflessly and until the end for the cause they had sworn to. Their creed valued courage in battle and a righteous cause.

Despite press coverage in England at the time and the building of memorials in India, the story of Saragarhi became overshadowed by the Tirah campaign. But the frontier would continue to be a crucial area of operations which the Sikhs took a key stake in leading up to and including the third Afghan War in 1919. To mark their contribution with the latter, a stained glass window dedicated to Sikhs was unveiled at the Indian Army Memorial Room at Royal Military Academy Sandhurst in 1971 by Field Marshal Claude Auchinleck[110].

Nonetheless, what should have been a story of bravery and valour recognised and repeated the world over has largely disappeared from public consciousness, perhaps because the Great War which followed seventeen years after the battle of Saragarhi consumed every element of research and interest in that period of history.

But it is with the 1914-18 conflict that we find the strongest indication of the legacy of the story of Saragarhi, as with the reputation of Sikhs now fully established as staunch and loyal to the British they were thrust into the heart of the action in Europe. Saragarhi can thus be seen as a point in time from whence the British not only valued and relied upon the Sikhs but came to count on them most out of all the various martial races.

The decision to deploy Indians of any kind in Europe was not a light one for the British, who perceived dangers in allowing native soldiers to fight on western soil. But Sikhs would be deployed in great numbers all over the globe in the various Indian Expeditionary Forces (IEF) that were sent to fight.

IEF A went to the Western Front and was vital in filling the gaps of the Allied defence in Flanders. IEF B and C served in East Africa, the Sikh princely states including Patiala and Kapurthala playing a key role in raising a fighting force of Imperial Service Troops. IEF D was sent to Mesopotamia where the mission changed from defending the oil supply for the British Navy to capturing Baghdad. IEF E served in Sinai and Palestine, while IEF F defended the vital Suez Canal route. IEF G was involved with the ill-fated campaign at Gallipoli alongside ANZAC forces. Sikhs were also found in Hong Kong, Singapore and in the Far East playing a crucial role; at Tsingtao in China the 36th Sikhs took part in a siege at the German controlled port.

Appreciation of the Sikh martial traditions and military value to the British can be seen in that they stood alongside them in every area of operations during the Great War, a sign of the special friendship that the two now enjoyed.

Conclusion

The heroism at Saragarhi is one which can easily draw parallels with other last stands, notably with the Spartans at Thermopylae or the British at Rorke's Drift. But what is so special about the soldiers involved at Saragarhi is that they were of a foreign land to their commanders whose nation's interests they were fighting to defend. The Sikhs fought for the British on the Samana, they were acting upon British interests during the period of the "Great Game" and for a foreign ruler they had no connection to whatsoever.

They fought because they had sworn an oath to do so and they were men of their word. They had joined the 36th Sikhs because they saw it as their martial duty to take on the service – the reasons they did so would have been personal to each individual soldier. Some wanted to earn a regular income and provide for their family, others might have seen it as an opportunity to do something different to the farm labouring their families had undertaken for generations. There would have been the romantics too, drawn to the idea of fighting the Pathans and defending India in the same way their forefathers had during the period of the Sikh Sardars such as Nawab Kapur Singh or Jassa Singh Ahluwalia. Others might have been more zealous about the Sikh faith and martial tradition, and seen any war against a common enemy as a righteous one.

The British too knew full well the benefit of raising the Sikhs and sending them to the frontier to fight the Pathans. The Frontier Force they raised for the purpose after the Anglo-Sikh Wars went through several reorganisations, and were expanded to ensure a steady body of fighting men could counter the threat during the "Great Game". As the Sikhs proved through their service that they were more than fully capable of the harsh realities of conflict in the rugged terrain, so too did they become emboldened to act bravely.

On the Samana, the 36th Sikhs were best placed to show this – and any of the men could have been despatched to man the Saragarhi outpost. The actions of the Sikhs there are unparalleled – faced with immense odds with a limited amount of ammunition and no chance of reinforcements, they didn't neglect their duties (as the Pathan levies at other outposts did) but stood firm and fought. But so too are the actions of their brethren at Gulistan worthy of praise, as despite being surrounded the Sikhs there volunteered to engage the enemy and embrace a certain death.

Havildar Ishar Singh showed strong leadership, no doubt inspired by the Sikh tenets, to lead his men to the bitter end. In remembering the words of Guru Gobind Singh, he and his men did not falter in performing righteous actions. They were not intimidated by the enemy, and with their mind fixed on God they knew they would soon meet their Creator. They sensed their mortal life was coming to an end at the small outpost, and so fought fiercely in battle. They were victorious because the story of their heroic deeds lives on. Their self-sacrifice was an example to others of how to live and how best to die. Their actions inspired the Sikhs in their regiment as well as others serving in British India.

Their heroics continue to inspire Indians today – officers at the regimental headquarters of 4 Sikh continue to be inspired by the images of Saragarhi. The battle lives on in the memory of the Sikh regiments in India, and to some extent military circles in Britain and elsewhere. But the true historic nature of the battle and its relevance today has been forgotten because of the disconnection in understanding why the Sikhs did what they did for the British. Sikhs today might find it difficult to acknowledge this sacrifice on the frontier at the height of Empire when they look at it through a post-independence prism. They might appreciate the Sikh fighting spirit and the ways in which they defended India but yet not fully comprehend why it has significance today.

But the story of Saragarhi does indeed provide strong relevance for Sikhs today – particular those in Britain and outside of India, as the reputation of their creed as faithful and loyal was created by the battle and the enduring contribution Sikhs made on the frontier and in the Great War ensured their reputation proceeded the community wherever they went in the world. This put Sikhs in a positive light when they subsequently migrated to all parts of the world, their turban identity kept in accordance with Sikh principles of not cutting hair made them instantly recognisable. And their hard work ethos and strong religious ethics meant they were valued as contributors to society. We can be thankful that to a large extent this view still exists today in places where the Diaspora has settled.

Within India, the battle honour which belongs to 4 Sikh continues to be observed in various ways – military halls have been named after the battle, articles are continuously written extolling the virtues of the brave Sikhs, and most importantly the 12th September is kept as a holiday during which prayers take place at regimental centres. Sikh soldiers who now serve India remember what their forebears did to defend the sub-continent against Pathan aggression and can take much pride in continuing their legacy through their service. Yet, outside of India the history of Sikhs on the frontier should be commemorated by all and Saragarhi day marked with similar festivities. This effort has begun to be made in the UK by various heritage organisations.

Those who follow Saragarhi should also seek an understanding of how the Sikhs were empowered to do what they did – fight bravely and be ever willing to be a sacrifice for their beliefs. It is through Khalsa initiation that Sikhs get their martial fervour, coupled with the deep spiritual belief in the message of the True Guru.

Understanding and then acting upon these teachings gave deeper purpose to the actions of the Sikh soldiers then – and can continue to inspire people of all backgrounds today to act in good faith and with virtue.

The best place to pay homage to this is at the two Saragarhi memorial Gurdwaras built in memory of the last stand by the British after the battle. Visiting the Harimandir Sahib at Amritsar is a pilgrimage every Sikh does – and the holy site attracts many non-Sikhs too. A short walk away from the complex is the Saragarhi Memorial Gurdwara, an important aspect of remembrance of the battle which every person who wants to understand the role of Saragarhi should visit as it was built in the religious centre of the Sikhs to inspire future generations. So too does the Memorial at Ferozepur provide a reminder of the strong Sikh ethics held by the Sikhs who fought, particularly as the *shabad* tablets contained at the site give a unique insight into the character of the saint-soldiers who fought.

Saragarhi is an ideal example of what the Sikh spirit is capable of when deployed for a higher purpose. In invoking the memory of Saragarhi, we can instantly think of selflessness and valour, but these qualities were demonstrated because of the adherence of the Sikh soldiers to the Khalsa code of conduct. They lived in accordance of the creed created by Guru Gobind Singh, and this meant abiding by their oath to fulfil their duty on the Samana and to fight their enemy without being intimidated. In this they observed the words of the Sikh national anthem and as a consequence found glory thereafter.

In detailing Saragarhi we must turn to historic research and evidence to find its deeper meaning otherwise we risk losing its value and replacing its wisdom with popular culture versions of the story propagated for reasons other than finding the truth. The battle might not be as well known as other last stands, but by being one which requires discovery it offers a fascinating prospect to those willing to venture out and try and find it - insight into how a small group from a martial race cemented the reputation of their people through service and self-sacrifice.

In January 1898, General William Lockhart applauded this "splendid conduct" of the Sikhs in a letter to Bhagat Lakshman Singh, celebrating a race of people who had gone from sworn enemies to most loyal friends: *"For no race have I more sincere regard than that which I entertain for the Sikhs who as enemies won our admiration half a century ago, and have since then furnished the forces of the Queen with thousands of gallant soldiers and men who have shown their heroism wherever there was fighting to be done.[111]"*

Lakshman Singh, whose names appears on the Lockhart address sent by leading Rawalpindi Sardars in January 1898 was an educationalist at the time teaching at the Gordon Mission School in Rawalpindi. The sign off he received from his correspondent deserves to be the final say on the matter as it is an enduring message that Sikhs should long continue to propagate when telling the story of Saragarhi: *"May the heroic national spirit of the Khalsa continue and flourish, and in future wars may Sikhs ever be found fighting as trusty comrades side by side with their British brothers-in-arms.[112]"*

Endnote

As this volume is revised for the 120th anniversary of Saragarhi, the writer and team at Dot Hyphen Productions (including creative director Manpreet Singh Talwar) have been working on telling this epic story in documentary format for worldwide release on the battle honour day of 12th September 2017.

The journey to make this new film has been a long one, it takes on board much of my research (much of which is contained within this book, but some yet unpublished); and it encompasses much time and effort spent in gaining never-before-seen archive, rare images and specialist insight from key experts into the various elements of the battle and its connected history.

For the first time we have also showcased the modern ruins of Saragarhi in tribal Pakistan in the film. The site is very different today, not much of the ruins of the archive images survive intact, but we do get a sense of their positions and standing from the footage.

We have also rediscovered the burial site of Lt Col John Haughton in Peshawar, which while much of the marble memorial has since gone the piece containing his name thankfully survives to show us where he is buried.

The work and effort undertaken and its connected research will be shared in due course, but rather than trying to cram it all into this volume I urge those interested to purchase the DVD of "Saragarhi: The True Story" to see for yourself how we have brought this history alive.

Let history inspire you to undertake great deeds!

J. Singh-Sohal

Soldiers from the 36th on the march during the Tirah campaign in 1897.

ਹਿੰਦ ਦੀ ਸਰਕਾਰ ਨੇ
ਇਹ ਇਮਾਰਤ ਸਿੱਖ ਦੀ ਫ਼ਤੀਰਿਪਲਟਣ
ਦੇ ਉਨ੍ਹਾਂ ਇੱਕੀ ਦੇਸੀ ਅਫ਼ਸਰਾਂ ਅਤੇ ਸਿਪਾਹੀਆਂ
ਦੀ ਯਾਦਗਾਰ ਵਿੱਚ ਜਿਨ੍ਹਾਂ ਦੇ ਨਾਉਂ ਹੇਠ ਲਿਖੇ ਹੋਏ
ਹਨ ਬਨਵਾਈ ਹੈ। ਇਸ ਲਈ ਜੋ ਇਨ੍ਹਾਂ ਬਹਾਦਰਾਂ ਦੀ
ਬਹਾਦਰੀ ਦਲੀਆ ਵਿੱਚ ਸਦਾ ਰੱਹੇ ਰਹੇ । ਜਿਨ੍ਹਾਂ ਨੇ
ਸਰਹੱਦੀ ਕਿਲੇ ਸਾਰਗੜ੍ਹੀ ਦੀ ਰਖੀ ਵਿੱਚ ਬਹੁਤ ਸਾਰੇ
ਦੁਸਮਨ ਦੇ ਨਾਲ ਲੜਦਿਆਂ ਹੋਇਆਂ ਬਹਵੀ ਸਿੱਤੰਬਰ
ਸਨ ੧੮੭੩ ਨੂੰ ਆਪਣੀ ਥਾਉਂ ਤੇ ਜਾਨਾਂ ਦੇ ਦਿੱਤੀਆਂ ਅਤੇ
ਇਸ ਤਰਾਂ ਆਪਣੀ ਮਹਾਰਾਣੀ ਕੈਸਰਏ ਹਿੰਦ ਦੇ ਨਾਲ
ਆਪਣੀ ਨਿਮਕ ਹਲਾਲੀ ਅਤੇ ਵਫ਼ਦਾਰੀ ਦਾ ਸਬੂਤ
ਦਿਖ ਦਿੱਤ ਅਤੇ ਲੜਾਈ ਦੇ ਮਦਾਨ ਵਿੱਚ ਸਿਖਾਂ ਦੀ
ਬੇਧੜਕ ਦਲੇਰੀ ਦੀ ਪਰਸਿੱਧੀ (ਮਸ਼ਹੂਰੀ) ਨੂੰ
ਕਾਇਮ ਰੱਖਿਆ ।

੧੬੫ ਹਵਲਦਾਰਈਸਰਸਿੰਘ
੩੩੨ ਨਾਯਕ ਨਾਲ ਸਿੰਘ   ੫੪੬ ਲੈਂ ਨਾਯਕ ਚੈਂਦਸਿੰਘ
੧੩੨੧ਸਿਪਾਹੀ ਸੁਧ ਸਿੰਘ   ੧੮੨ ਸਿਪਾਹੀ ਸਾਹਿਬਸਿੰਘ
੪੯੨ " ਉੱਤਮਸਿੰਘ   ੨੮੭ " ਰਾਮਸਿੰਘ
੩੫੯ " ਹੀਰਾਸਿੰਘ   ੬੮੭ " ਦਯਾਸਿੰਘ
੭੯੧ " ਭੋਲਾਸਿੰਘ   ੬੦ " ਜੀਵਨਸਿੰਘ
੮੩੪ " ਨਰਾਯਣ ਸਿੰ.   ੮੧੪ " ਗੁਰਮੁਖਸਿੰਘ
੮੭੧ " ਜੀਵਨ ਸਿੰਘ   ੧੭੩੩ " ਗੁਰਮੁਖਸਿੰਘ
੧੬੩ " ਰਾਮਸਿੰਘ   ੧੩੫੭ " ਭਗਵਾਨ ਸਿੰਘ
੧੨੬੫ " ਭਗਵਾਨਸਿੰਘ   ੧੫੫੬ " ਬੂਟਾਸਿੰਘ
੧੬੫੧ " ਜੀਵਾ ਸਿੰਘ   ੧੨੨੧ " ਨੰਦਸਿੰਘ

THE
GOVERNMENT OF INDIA
HAVE CAUSED
THIS MEMORIAL TO BE ERECTED
TO THE MEMORY OF THE TWENTY ONE
NON COMMISSIONED OFFICERS AND MEN
OF THE 36TH SIKHS
WHOSE NAMES ARE ENGRAVED BELOW
AS A PERPETUAL RECORD OF THE HEROISM
SHEWN BY THESE GALLANT SOLDIERS
WHO DIED AT THEIR POSTS
IN THE DEFENCE OF THE FRONTIER FORT
OF SARAGARHI
ON THE 12TH SEPTEMBER 1897
FIGHTING AGAINST OVERWHELMING NUMBERS
THUS PROVING THEIR LOYALTY AND DEVOTION
TO THEIR SOVEREIGN
THE QUEEN EMPRESS OF INDIA
AND GLORIOUSLY MAINTAINING
THE REPUTATION OF THE SIKHS
FOR UNFLINCHING COURAGE
ON THE FIELD OF BATTLE

165 HAVILDAR ISHAR SINGH
332 NAIK LALL SINGH   546 L NAIK CHANDA SINGH
1321 SEPOY SUDH SINGH 182 SEPOY SAHIB SINGH
492 D' UTTAM SINGH   287 D' RAM SINGH
359 D' HIRA SINGH   687 D' DAYA SINGH
791 D' BHOLA SINGH   60 D' JIWAN SINGH
834 D' NARAIN SINGH   814 D' GURMUKH SINGH
871 D' JIWAN SINGH   1733 D' GURMUKH SINGH
163 H' RAM SINGH   1357 D' BHAGWAN SINGH
1265 D' BHAGWAN SINGH 1556 D' BUTA SINGH
1651 D' JIWA SINGH   1221 D' NAND SINGH

Saragarhi Memorial Gurdwara, previous page, opened in April 1902 in Amritsar to remind the Sikhs of their bravery in their spiritual capital. Behind it now looms a new hostel for foreign visitors to Harimandi Sahib.

Above and right show the tablets on the Gurdwara walls detailing the names and bravery of the twenty-one in Gurmukhi and English.

Canon above is one of several outside Saragarhi Gurdwara Ferozpur, unveiled in January 1904, shown on pages 101 and 102.

Below: descendants of the Saragarhi Sikhs being honoured during the centenary anniversary in 1997.

Saragarhi Day commemorations are held every year by Sikh Regiments in India. Here, 4 Sikh Regiment mark the event in September 2013.

NISCHE KAR APNI JEET KARON

About The Author

Captain Jagjeet Singh-Sohal (or Jay) is a communications consultant, presenter and filmmaker, as well as a British Army Reservist.

He has been researching the story of Saragarhi since 2010 and in 2013 founded the annual "Saragarhi Day" comemmoration in the UK. He is the founder and Chairman of the "WW1 Sikh Memorial" Britain'first monument to Sikh servicelocated at the National Memorial Arboretum.

A former journalist he has output produced live international stories at Sky News and reported at ITV regional newsrooms.

Jay makes independent films through "Dot Hyphen Productions" which bring the Sikh story to mainstream audiences. This includes the "Turbanology" project and the "Sikhs At War" series of online films exploring the historic contribution made during the world wars.

For further reading and online films visit: www.sikhsatwar.info

Contributors:

Harjinder Singh (researcher)
Harjinder has a long history of serving the Sikh community, and has worked in many voluntary organisations in community development and in the public sector as a commissioner of services. He chairs "Akaal Publishers" writing, editing and translating tracts and books; and runs a tuition company.

Jag Lall (cover artist)
Jag Lall's artwork has featured in several creative media ranging from books, paintings, short films and comic books. An expressive and emotive painter, Jag also works in several mediums from acrylics to Photoshop and pen and ink. Jag continually illustrates artwork in an effort to bridge cultural barriers.

Appendices

Select Saragarhi articles sourced from our blog on www.sikhsatwar.info

Lt Col John Haughton, Commander 36th Sikhs

It was an early start and long drive to Leicestershire earlier this month when we set out on a pilgrimage to immerse ourselves in the life of a man whose service to his country would earn him the description of 'a hero of Tirah'.

Lt Col John Haughton was the commander of the 36th Sikhs on the Samana which in 1897 was the scene of a tribal uprising that would earn his regiment a battle honour. It would, of course, also be where the battle of Saragarhi took place and where 21 Sikhs would defend the small signalling post against the onslaught of 10,000 enemy tribesmen.

Haughton commanded his men from Fort Lockhart during the uprising, deploying the 21 to Saragarhi as well as reinforcing Fort Gulistan which was also under attack. His leadership was exceptional and was a testament to an officer who knew his men, had studied tactics and the local geography and knew how to counter the enemy.

Our trip to Leicestershire was with the aim of finding out and documenting more about Haughton's character, about his Victorian education at Uppingham, a public school founded in 1584; and to see the memorial dedicated to his life and sacrifice.

It was a trip three years in the making, having discovered the connection during my research for my book I'd been in contact with the school but unable to make the trek for various reasons until now. It was well worth it, as you'll see.

Haughton was born in August 1852 in India – where his father, Lt-Gen John Colpoys Haughton, was stationed. The General had served with the 31st Bengal infantry in the first Afghan war (1839-42) and distinguished himself during the defence of Charikar in 1841. A career-soldier and administrator, Haughton raised a family in India, his son John was born in August 1852 at Chota Nagpur.

There John Haughton would remain until August 1865, when at the age of 13 he was sent back to Britain to attend school. It was believed that public schools such as Uppingham ought to have an important part in the military training of the youth of the upper and middle classes.

Haughton, though while having a strong military figure in his father, did not distinguish himself during his schooling as evidenced in his reports. At 17 he went to a crammer to prepare for the entrance exam at Royal Military Academy Sandhurst, which he passed first time. He passed out in 1871 and was gazetted with the 1st Bn 24th Foot (later the South Wales Borderers). His father applied for John to be gazetted to a regiment in India, and he joined the 72nd Highlanders, which was stationed in Peshawar.

He later helped raise the 35th Sikhs in Ferozepur in May 1887 and remained with it before being brevetted as Lt Colonel to its sister-regiment the 36th, taking over command in June 1894. From April 1895 to December 1896 the regiment remained in Peshawar, before then marching onto the Samana to occupy the Forts and posts there.

Thereafter, Haughton led the 36th Sikhs during the Tirah Expedition, where it joined the 4th Brigade in protecting the right flank of the advancing troops on the Samana Suk. From the Dargai heights to the Maidan Valley, the 36th made the trek to subdue the Afridi and Orakzai tribes.

It was on 29th January 1898, five months after Saragarhi, that Haughton would fall while in battle. He was tasked to recce caves beyond the Shinkamar pass, but a misunderstanding in orders led to his party of Sikhs being exposed from the rear. The Pathans advanced and Haughton ordered his men to fix bayonets and fire the last of their ammunition. But the order to charge never came, a sniper hit Haughton with a bullet to the head, and he died.

Haughton would be buried at a British cemetery in Peshawar, and his brother officers in the 35th and 36th would raise a memorial plaque in his honour at the school chapel at Uppingham. The plaque would state: "Sacred to the memory of Lt. Col. John Haughton, Commandant of the 36th Sikhs who was killed in action at the Shinkamar pass N.W. Frontier of India 29th January 1898 while boldly defending a position to the last against overwhelming odds. This brass is erected by his brother officers of the 35th and 36th Sikhs."

His biographer Major A.C Yates writes of Haughton's qualities that he had a high sense of duty, strong religious feeling, staunchness, cool courage and a readiness to sacrifice himself. Much of the detail of his life and service can be found in "A Hero of Tirah" which I recommend for further reading.

Having known about his service and sacrifice, the trip to Uppingham gave us a deeper understanding of his education, and the values he gained from it. It was a rare treat to see such a prestigious place and to speak to an expert in the archivist Jerry Rudman, an interview of which we look forward to bringing to you in due course. And it was a remarkable opportunity to share Haughton's story with the school, who knew little of what happened to their old boy after he left.

Saragarhi's lost link to Sheffield

** Our immense gratitude to Don Nicolson from Olde Edwardian's for providing primary source material used within this article.**

It is a rewarding journey to research into a history, simply to discover new and fascinating connections. It can be a true delight when one interesting thread of thought, once tugged at, unravels a whole new web of untold stories.

This is just what happened during a Christmas luncheon I attended in Westminster. I sat down opposite someone who had a strong connection to my interest in Saragarhi. Having mentioned I had written a book and explaining what it was about, my acquaintance revealed his grandfather had served during Tirah! He would have certainly crossed through the Samana at the time of the epic battle and would have seen the small ruined outpost which was defended by 21 valiant Sikhs.

I came away from the lunch with a new thread to pull at, and as I pursued this link I came across something I had yet to discover – a wonderful connection between Saragarhi ...and Sheffield! This story is being told below for the first time, and I hope it will trigger more lost connections (and hopefully more primary accounts) to be found.

On the frontier, British soldiers and officers formed a part of the Tirah Expeditionary Force, which was sent in 1897 after the Samana posts were attached to subdue the unruly tribes who had been incited by their Mullahs to wage holy war.

111

One such young officer was 22 year old Bernard Haslam of the Royal Engineers who wrote to his uncle about the experience and of what he saw. The uncle in question was the Rev. A.B. Haslam the headmaster of Sheffield Grammar, and extracts of the letters written from Fort Lockhart in August and September 1897 were duly published in the school newspaper.

The account begins on the 26th July 1897 with a brief description of the Samana, and the revelation that "I shall, I suppose, mess with the 36th Sikhs". Haslam would be dining with the Sikh soldiers. He further adds "I am looking forward to a glorious time out there!."

Some weeks later on the 7th August, Haslam arrives at Fort Lockhart after a three hour journey on ponies, having set out from Hangu at 5.30am.

A week later he writes about the mountain conditions making everything damp but there is pleasantry also. "I had a great game of hockey yesterday" he writes. "Four of the officers of the 36th Sikhs and myself and some native officers and sepoys from the regiment were playing. Many of these played with legs bare to the knee, and some with bare feet. They were uncommonly good…"

By the 29th August, things are hotting up on the frontier with the nearby Shinwari post taken and burnt. Our officer describes how the Sikhs are garrisoning other posts and these are "far stronger" because of it, more so than the posts manned by border police – tribal levies of Pathans that often fled or refused to fight when confronted by their brethren.

Let us now turn to the fateful day of the 12th September, when Saragarhi was attacked and destroyed. Haslam was there and describes the dramatic events as thousands upon thousands of enemy tribesmen attacked the frontier post of Gulistan.

Here is the extract in full:

Fort Lockhart, 12th Sept.

The General (Yeatman Biggs) and staff came up here the other day but left yesterday evening. We heard them firing all night, but just now (11 a.m.) all is quiet, though we can see the enemy's standards two miles off in each direction. Oh for a field gun!

Last Friday Gulistan was rather heavily attacked at 2 p.m. Colonel Haughton and I and 50 men marched over, arriving about 5-30. We met with some volleys from a village across the valley, but no one was touched .Three men were slightly wounded at Gulistan when we arrived, and Pratt had been shot through the helmet, but was himself untouched. Fire continued till 2 a.m. when it practically ceased till 8 a.m.; then it began again and continued till noon. We then got a couple of volleys into the dense mass of men at 1,200 yards distance where they thought themselves out of range. We killed two or three and frightened the rest so much that they cleared off, and we returned here at 5 p.m.

Thereafter, Haslam gives another letter with further details of the events as he saw them at Saragarhi. This below is a remarkable first hand account which gives some unbelievable insight into what the 21 Sikhs at Saragarhi faced against the 10,000 enemy they stood against. It verifies that: i) the commander Lt Col John Haughton tried to relieve the garrison ii) helio messages were still being signalled up to the point that the post was overrun iii) one Sikh sentry killed 20 enemy, with 200 in total believed killed (the actual number is 180).

The extract reads:

Colonel Haughton came up to me and said that he and the Adjutant were going out with 50 men to create a diversion in favour of Saragheri, which had been fighting hard and lost four or five men out of 21; (this we knew by heliograph message). He therefore left me in charge with 120 men of the 36th and about 24 Sikh of the Royal Irish (left behind by the General). It wasn't nice being left in that way, for when I said "Good-bye" to the two of them I hardly expected to see them both back. I went up on the parapet of the fort and had got the Royal Irish up, as they had magazine rifles- (the Sikhs have only Martinis)- to cover the Colonel with long range fire when he returned. Luckily I watched Saragheri through the long telescope, and before our party had gone more than half-a-mile of the two miles I saw the Orakzais rush from inside on to the parapet of Saragheri. I had the retreat sounded, and Colonel Haughton came back. Next morning, it was in ruins. It appears that the wooden door had been simply riddled with bullets till it collapsed and the tribesmen walked in. The sentry killed 20 of them, and all the wounded fired from their beds. Rumours say that 200 of the enemy were killed. The signaller alone was kep alive-not by any fault of his, for any Sikh would shoot himself rather than fall into the hands of a Pathan. He was signalling to the last, and probably his rifle was taken before he had a chance of using it on himself. Two-thirds of the Afridi Lashkar were said to be there as well as the Orakzais; and the impetuous nature of the attack was, I believe, due to the rivalry between the tribes. After that a still more determined attack was made on Gulistan, and was continued until we – the General and ourselves – relieved it at mid-day on Tuesday."

But this account also presents a couple of factual inaccuracies from the writers point of view, which are nonetheless explainable. Firstly, he did not see the wall on the opposite end fall in from where two tribesmen were digging (this was observed from Gulistan). Secondly, the idea of the tribesmen walking in sounds too casual when we know there was hand-to-hand fighting with those few Sikhs remaining when the post was rushed for the final time.

Also, the account given of what befell the signaller Gurmukh Singh does not clear up what exactly happened. I suggest he did indeed shoot himself rather than fall into enemy hands and this is based on the account of senior officers. But this version states he was "kept alive" and that it is "probable" his rifle was taken before he had a chance of using it on himself. Does this mean he fell prisoner? Or his weapon was somehow lost? Or pulled from him, perhaps in a fight? There is still much left unanswered, which leaves a mystery of exactly what happened, yet we can make educated assumptions with the sources we have based on what we do know of the Sikh soldier of that time.

This is a fantastic find, an historic eye witness account that truly gives more details about the fateful events on the Samana – and it will no doubt help in our factual understanding of what happened at Saragarhi, and hopefully inspire greater acts of such devotion to a just cause.

The fate that befell Bernard Haslam was akin to that of many other young British men. After his service on the frontier he would find himself fighting for his country during the Great War. He died not in India or the Western Front but modern day Iran, on 26 August 1918 aged 43 during the Persian campaign. He is named on the Tehran Memorial, details of which can be found from the CWGC website.

Finally, I end with a request to readers who have connections to Tirah to get in touch. I'd love to hear more such stories and hopefully continue to share this largely forgotten but highly relevant history with our wider audience.

The Indian Order of Merit

The Order of Merit (IOM) is the oldest military decoration for gallantry, being constituted in 1837. It was awarded to native Indians in three classes, and was the de factor equivalent of the Victoria Cross until Indians became eligible for the VC in 1911.

The order was first given to a soldier for a brave act at class III, with subsequent acts that were recognised eligible for class II then class I. And so an IOM at the upper 1st class was the equivalent of a Victoria Cross with two bars.

The India Medal 1896 – 1902

This is the India Medal 1895 – 1902, and it was awarded for campaigns on the Punjab Frontier, Chitral, Malakand and later Waziristan.

It was also given for the Samana – where the battle of Saragarhi took place in 1897, and Tirah the expedition that occurred thereafter.

Each medal with the clasps depicting the area of conflict the soldier or officer served tells a story, one of how the unruly frontier was policed and controlled during the Great Game.

Appendix A: The Punjab Frontier Force

The military defence of the frontier was, except one district, entrusted to the Punjab Frontier Force under the immediate orders of the Lieutenant Governor of the province. The force consisted of:

4 Regiments of Punjab Cavalry
1 Regiment of Corps of Guides
4 Mountain Batteries of Artillery
4 Regiments of Sikh Infantry
5 Regiments of Punjab Infantry
1 Regiment of Gurkhas.

The mixed Punjab regiments would have consisted of two companies each of Sikhs, Punjabi Mussalmans and Hindus.

Each regiment of Punjab Cavalry consisted of six troops in three squadrons, amounting to 550 all native ranks.

Each regiment of infantry consisted of eight companies, amounting to 832 all native ranks.

Appendix B: The 1897 Order of Merit list

The twenty-one Sikhs who laid down their lives during the Battle of Saragarhi were posthumously awarded the Indian Order of Merit, third class. They were:

Havildar Ishar Singh (regimental number 165)
Naik Lal Singh (332)
Lance Naik Chanda Singh (546)
Sepoy Sundar Singh (1321)
Sepoy Ram Singh (287)
Sepoy Uttar Singh (492)
Sepoy Sahib Singh (182)
Sepoy Hira Singh (359)
Sepoy Daya Singh (687)
Sepoy Jivan Singh (760)
Sepoy Bhola Singh (791)
Sepoy Narayan Singh (834)
Sepoy Gurmukh Singh (814)
Sepoy Jivan Singh (871)
Sepoy Gurmukh Singh (1733)
Sepoy Ram Singh (163)
Sepoy Bhagwan Singh (1257)
Sepoy Bhagwan Singh (1265)
Sepoy Buta Singh (1556)
Sepoy Jivan Singh (1651)
Sepoy Nand Singh (1221)

The following native troops from the 36th Sikhs were also awarded the Indian Order of Merit for their special acts of gallantry on the Samana:

Havildar Kala Singh (63)
Havildar Sunder Singh (755)
Lance Naik Sada Singh (807)
Lance Naik Harnam Singh (817)

Lance Nail Dewa Singh (1177)
Lance Naik Jiwan Singh (939)
Sepoy Hansa Singh (1196)
Sepoy Sundar Singh (330)
Sepoy Bhola Singh (383)
Sepoy Gurmukh Singh (1201)
Sepoy Sobha Singh (1288)
Sepoy Jiwan Singh (1354)
Sepoy Wariam Singh (1380)
Sepoy Ghulla Singh (1146)
Sepoy Kala Singh (1123)
Sepoy Attar Singh (1078)
Sepoy Sujan Singh (1046)
Sepoy Chajja Singh (1603)
Sepoy Badan Singh (1369)
Sepoy Phuman Singh (1597)
Sepoy Thaman Singh (1741)
Sepoy Sawan Singh (1066)
Sepoy Ghuna Singh (1600)
Sepoy Bhagwan Singh (1588)
Sepoy Harnam Singh (1589)
Sepoy Sher Singh (368)
Sepoy Ralla Singh (1632)
Sepoy Mihan Singh (1167 – 5th Punjabis)
Sepoy Hira Singh (1183)
Sepoy Natha Singh (1539)
Sepoy Jawahir Singh (1338)
Sepoy Basawa Singh (907)
Sepoy Bela Singh (1295)

Appendix C: Newspaper Coverage

C1: 12th February 1898

"The Commander-in-Chief in forwarding despatches from the late Major-General Yeatman-Biggs describing the measures taken by that officer to repel attacks made by the Afridis and Orakzais on our frontier posts on the Samana range in August and September 1897... says:

'His Excellency is of opinion that the operations in question were well planned and skilfully carried out. The march to the relief of Gulistan was performed under very trying circumstances, owing to the heat and to a great scarcity of water en route; but the force successfully accomplished its object with the same gallantry and cheerfulness as have been evinced on every occasion by our troops during the various operations which have recently taken place on the North-West Frontier."

"The Commander-in-Chief wishes to draw attention to the admirable conduct and steadiness of the 36th Sikhs, during the attack on the various posts held by that regiment on the Samana range. At Sangar the small garrison made a sortie and gallantly captured a standard from the enemy, while the brilliant defence of Fort Gulistan by the detachment under the command of Major Des Voeux reflects the greatest credit on that officer and the garrison of the post. The Government of India will, His Excellency is assured, appreciate fully the intrepid manner in which the late Havildar Kala Sing (sic)led the sortie from the Gulistan Fort, and also the conduct of Havildar Sundar Singh, who assisted his comrades at a critical moment."

Particular reference was made to Saragarhi in the article:

"The Commander-in-Chief deeply regrets the loss of the garrison of Saragarhi, a post held by twenty-one men of the 36th Sikhs, and he wishes to record his admiration of the heroism shown by those gallant soldiers. Fighting against overwhelming numbers they died at their

post, thus proving their loyalty and devotion to their sovereign, while upholding to the last the traditional bravery of the Sikh nation..."

C2: The Times also carried the following despatch, which also appeared in the London Gazette on 11th February 1898:

"The Governor-General in Council desires especially to express his admiration of the brilliant defence of Fort Gulistan by the 36th Sikhs, and of the post of Saragarhi by a party of 20 men of the same regiment under the command of Havildar Ishar Singh who died fighting to the last, displaying a heroic devotion which has never been surpassed in the annals of the Indian Army."

C3: 13th July 1898

"Her Majesty's Government especially desire to record their high appreciation of the gallant conduct and admirable qualities of the British and native commissioned, warrant and N-C officers and privates of her Majesty's forces engaged in the campaign [on the frontier]... They especially desire to record their admiration of the 36th Sikhs, who were all killed fighting to the last in defence of the post of Saragarhi..."

"The Secretary of State for India has sanctioned the issue of a gratuity to all officers, N-C officers and men, including the Imperial Service troops, engaged in the recent operations on the North Western Frontier. The gratuity will be issued at the rate of Rs. 24 per share for the British and Rs. 12 for native soldiers, according to the rank of the recipient, and will be admissible to the heirs of those killed in action or who died of disease during the operations."

From a Times Correspondent reporting from Allahabad on 6th April, covering Viceroy's speech at Lahore:

"Replying on the same day to a Sikh deputation, Lord Curzon made a stirring speech, eulogizing the Sikh race. He said:-

"The Sikh soldiers of the Army of the Queen has given many illustrations of heroic courage in 50 years fighting for the British Raj since the time, now nearly forgotten, which they fought so well against us, so that the name of your race has become almost synonymous in the English language with traditions of desperate courage and unflinching loyalty. There are many qualities required to constitute the ideal soldier – bravery, endurance, a certain aptitude of intellect, discipline – but I am not sure that above them all I would not disregard of self that impels a man to die at his post, as the Sikhs did at Saragarhi, unmurmuring, even happy, in fighting against overwhelming odds.

When I visited Lyallpur on Monday I was received by veterans of your race, pensioners of the native army on whose bosoms were the Queen's medals recording prowess in China, Abyssinia, Egypt, Burma and Afghanistan – no mean synopsis of the range of action of the Sikh soldiers. Never may the day arise when the British Government, in time of need, cannot rely upon his stanch unquestionable service!

I think you know we are neither unconscious of, nor ungrateful for, the long and honourable record of Sikh allegiance. If proofs were needed, I might refer to the monument about to be erected at Amritsar of the Sikh soldiers of the 36th Regiment who gave up their lives at Saragarhi, while the popular appreciation of that heroic incident will be shown by the further memorial to be erected by public subscription at Firozpur [sic]. These two monuments will testify to later ages at once the valour of your race and the gratitude of mine. Nevertheless, in the modern world military virtues, however pre-eminent, are not the only requisite for the preservation of national existence, and you have wisely realised that if you are to hold your own with the wise, populous, and erudite peoples among whom you may be placed you must provide your families with an education comparable with theirs, I am pleased to learn that Khalsa College has already attained a high standard of excellence..."

C5: 13th November 1901

"The following is the inscription for the Saragarhi memorial at Fort Lockhart, which it is proposed to place also on the tablets at Amritsar:-

"The Government of India have caused this memorial to be erected to the memory of 21 non-commissioned officers and men of the 36th Sikhs, whose names are engraved below as a perpetual record of the heroism shown by these gallant soldiers who died at their posts in the defence of the frontier post Saragarhi, September 12th 1897, fighting against overwhelming numbers and thus proving their loyalty and devotion to the Sovereign Queen-Empress of India, and gloriously maintaining the reputation of the Sikhs for unflinching courage on the field of battle."

Then follow the names.

It will be remembered that in the autumn of 1897, when the Orakzai Afridis rose, they attacked the Saragarhi post on the Samana.

Saragarhi fell after a heroic defence, the enemy having mined the tower before the late Gen. Sir Penn Symons could sufficiently reinforce the Samana range."

C6: 17th April 1902

"Memorial to Sikh Soldiers

Bombay, April 16

General Sir Arthur Power Palmer, the Commander-in-Chief, yesterday unveiled the Saragarhi memorial at Amritsar, in the presence of the Lieutenant-Governor and other officials, the officers of the Punjab district, and representatives of all the Sikh regiments. The ceremony was most impressive.

After referring to the unavoidable absence of Lord Curzon, the Commander-in-Chief said:

"The memorial is the outcome of the spontaneous appreciation of the gallantry of a representative detachment of the Sikh nation, proving that they possess one of the finest of soldierly characteristics – namely, that they prefer death to surrender."

Sir Arthur Palmer mentioned a few details of the incident giving rise to the memorial. He felt, he said, that the conduct displayed by the 21 men of the 36th Sikh Regiment whose names were inscribed on the memorial was characteristic of the nation's traditions. It should be kept as an example to others, in order to show how brave men should behave when facing fearful odds. He referred to the stanchness [sic] of the Sikhs at the time of the Indian Mutiny, and especially mentioned the services of the grand-father of the present chief of Kapurthala, who took a contingent to Jalandhar and Ondh [sic]. The memorial, said the Commander-in-Chief in conclusion, was erected at the headquarters of the Sikh religion, in order that as long as the British rule lasted the brave Sikh soldiers of the King might realize that their deeds would never be forgotten."

C7: 1st November 1926

Viceroy's visit to Frontier forts on 29th October 1926:

"Lady Irwin, on leaving Kohat, motored to Hangu, nearly 40 miles towards the beginning of the Kurram Valley, down which the Afghan Army came in 1919, and from Hangu she went to Fort Lockhart on Samana Hill, which became famous in 1897 from the heroic defence of the little Saragarhi post adjacent by a detachment of the old 36th Sikhs, which is commemorated by a marble tablet in the Westminster Abbey of the Sikhs, the Golden Temple of Amritsar."

C8: 4th August 1947

"Service Notices.

36th Sikhs (4 Bn The Sikh Regt.). It is proposed to hold a Lunch on Saragarhi Day (12th September 1947) – Will all wishing attend write Brigadier Purves, 17 Cutcliffe Place, Bedford."

Appendix D: Address to General Sir William Lockhart KCB KCSI

Respected Sir,

We crave leave to respectfully approach you and present you with this our humble address on behalf of the local Sikh community, and to say that it is no small gratification to us that we should have an opportunity to perform such a pleasing duty.

Of all the people inhabiting the continent of India the Khalsa has been foremost in upholding the glory of the British arms, through the world, and its representatives in the largest military station in Her Majesty's Indian Empire, maybe excused if they should wait upon you to give an expression to their feelings of admiration at the gallantry displayed by your troops during the recent campaign in Tirah. The mission of the British people and the Khalsa is alike. The British have done most in civilizing humanity, and the Khalsa has spilt its best blood, during the last 200 years, for rendering the same service to the people of this country. It has unfetted their minds and unshackled their limbs. It has brought into play energies lying dormant for ages. It has taught the oppressed millions to shake off tyranny of every form and description. The subjugation of the tribes on the North West Frontier is the rescuing of humanity from barbarism and blessed are they to whose lot this service falls. Before the advent of the British rule into this country the Khalsa was employed in this noble work and it is its particular good fortune that it should be associated with the British in the continuance of to the same.

The recent campaign has taught, among others, two important lessons. It has convinced the misguided people of Tirah that insult to Britain's name cannot go unpunished. It has also made it possible for the Saragarhi martyrs to prove by their example that in time of need the Sikhs would die to a man in service of Her Most Gracious Majesty the Queen Empress, and it has enabled the Government and the non-official European community, in this country, to help the Saragarhi Memorial movement and thus practically acknowledge the existence of a tie of mutual regard and fellowship. This being the case it is but natural that the Sikhs should wish success to the British arms and feel interested in the general that leads their people to victory over their ancient foes. Personally to you our hearty thanks are due for the care and anxiety with which you watch the interests of our community and it is with a feeling of no small delight that we accord you a hearty welcome on your safe return in our midst. We humbly pray that Providence may be graciously pleased to grant you health and happiness, all your life, and success in your future undertakings.

We beg to remain, respect Sir,
Your obedient servant

Signed by leading Sikh Sardars

Rawal Pindi:
8th January 1898

Picture Credits

Crest of the 36th Sikhs by Jag Lall: p6

Images courtesy of 4 Sikh archives, Chandigarh: p22, 23, 61, 62, 63, 64

Courtesy of Neil Aspinshaw, p24

Image Landsat US Department of State Geographer, Image © 2013 Digital Globe © 2013 Google: p19, 20, 21

© The British Library Board: p56, 57, 58, 59, 60

© Rene Bull, Black and White Publishing Co, London: p99

Photographs by Harjinder Singh: p100, 101, 102

Courtesy of Gurinderpal Singh: p104

Courtesy of Lt General H.S Panag: p105

Authors collection: p108, 110, 111, 116

References

[1] The Campaign in Tirah: An Account of the expedition against the Orakzais and Afridis; Col H.D Hutchinson, Lancer, p12

[2] Turkestan included modern day Turkmenistan, Kazakhstan, Uzbekistan, Kyrgyzstan and Xinjiang

[3] Afghanistan 1919: An Account of Operations in the Third Afghan War; George Molesworth, p17

[4] Operations against the Orakzai Tribe on the Miranzai Frontiers under the command of Brigadier-General Sir W.S.A Lockhart in 1891, by Capt. A.H Mason, Simla, 1891, p18

[5] Ibid p23

[6] Ibid p26

[7] Ibid p29

[8] The Morning Post newspaper, The Indian Frontier Expedition, 22 April 1891

[9] Operations against the Orakzai Tribe on the Miranzai Frontiers under the command of Brigadier-General Sir W.S.A Lockhart in 1891, by Capt. A.H Mason, Simla, 1891, p36 7

[10] Ibid, p xxxvi, appendix T

[11] Ibid, p xxxvi, appendix T

[12] Ibid

[13] Ibid

[14] Lt-Col John Haughton, Commandant of the 36th Sikhs; A hero of Tirah, a memoir; A.C Yate, 1900, p117

[15] Ibid p118

[16] Ibid

[17] Operations against the Orakzai Tribe on the Miranzai Frontiers under the command of Brigadier-General Sir W.S.A Lockhart in 1891, by Capt. A.H Mason, Simla, 1891, p xxxvi, appendix T

[18] Ibid

[19] Ibid

[20] Lt-Col John Haughton, Commandant of the 36th Sikhs; A hero of Tirah, a memoir; A.C Yate, 1900, p117

[21] Ibid, p118

[22] Operations against the Orakzai Tribe on the Miranzai Frontiers under the command of Brigadier-General Sir W.S.A Lockhart in 1891, by Capt. A.H Mason, Simla, 1891, appendix Y

[23] The Heliograph, Major A G Harfield, p2

[24] Ibid

[25] Ibid

[26] Turbanology: Guide to Sikh Identity; Jay Singh-Sohal, Dot Hyphen Publishers, 2012, p52

[27] Ibid, p52

[28] Ibid

[29] Ibid, p56

[30] Sri Gur Panth Parkash, Rattan Singh Bhangoo, English translation by Kulwant Singh, 2006, Institute of Sikh Studies, Chandigarh, p126

[31] The Turban: Symbol of Sikh Identity, W.H McLeod in Sikh identity: continuity and change; McLeod, Singh, Barrier et al, Ann Arbor; MI, New Delhi; Manohar; 1999, p60

[32] A record of the expeditions against the North-West Frontier tribes since the annexation of the Punjab, Lt Col W.H. Paget, 1873, London

[33] The Story of the Malakand Field Force, Winston Churchill, 1898

[34] Sepoys in the Trenches: The Indian Corps on the Western Front 1914-15; Gordon Corrigan, Spellmount, p2

[35] Ibid, p2

[36] Ibid, p3

[37] The Indian army and the king's enemies 1900 – 1947; Chevenix Trench, Thames & Hudson 1967, p11

[38] Sepoys in the Trenches: The Indian Corps on the Western Front 1914-15; Gordon Corrigan, Spellmount, p5

[39] The Indian army and the king's enemies 1900 – 1947; Chevenix Trench, Thames & Hudson 1967, p11

[40] The Story of the Malakand Field Force, Winston Churchill, 1898

[41] Ibid

[42] Presentation of Standards and Colours By His Royal Highness The Prince of Wales, 11 March 1922, Rawalpindi, p11

[43] Saragarhi Battalion: Ashes to Glory, History of the 4th Battalion the Sikh Regiment; Col. Kanwaljit Singh & Maj. H.S Ahluwalia, Lancer New Delhi, p14

[44] Ibid

[45] Ibid

[46] The British were successful in playing to the strengths of the various castes and religious groupings within India and recruited within these divisions to ensure homogeneity of units for specific tasks. Jatt Sikh companies were deployed in areas where hardships and fighting were intense, while Mazbi Sikhs were recruited for their intellect and specialists skills. Mixed caste units and mixed religious unites were also raised and utilised where needed.

[47] Lt-Col John Haughton, Commandant of the 36th Sikhs; A hero of Tirah, a memoir; A.C Yate, 1900, p114

[48] Presentation of Standards and Colours By His Royal Highness The Prince of Wales, 11 March 1922, Rawalpindi, p11

[49] Presentation of Standards and Colours By His Royal Highness The Prince of Wales, 11 March 1922, Rawalpindi, p11

[50] Indian Army List of January 1897, p374

[51] Saragarhi Battalion: Ashes to Glory, History of the 4th Battalion the Sikh Regiment; Col. Kanwaljit Singh & Maj. H.S Ahluwalia, Lancer New Delhi, p17

[52] Ibid, p19

[53] Information on the Saragarhi soldiers and their descendents provided by researcher Gurinderpal Singh

[54] The Khyber Rifles: From the British Raj to Al Qaeda; Jules Stewart, Sutton Publishing, p20

[55] Afghanistan 1919: An Account of Operations in the Third Afghan War; George Molesworth, p17

The Campaign in Tirah: An Account of the expedition against the Orakzais and Afridis; Col H.D Hutchinson, Lancer, p4-5

[57] Ibid, p12

[58] Ibid, appendix C

[59] Operations against the Orakzai Tribe on the Miranzai Frontiers under the command of Brigadier-General Sir W.S.A Lockhart in 1891, by Capt. A.H Mason, Simla, 1891, appendix K

[60] The Campaign in Tirah: An Account of the expedition against the Orakzais and Afridis; Col H.D Hutchinson, Lancer, p18

[61] Lt-Col John Haughton, Commandant of the 36th Sikhs; A hero of Tirah, a memoir; A.C Yate, 1900, p118 - 126

[62] Operations against the Orakzai Tribe on the Miranzai Frontiers under the command of Brigadier-General Sir W.S.A Lockhart in 1891, by Capt. A.H Mason, Simla, 1891, p51

[63] Ibid

[64] Ibid

[65] Ibid p52

[66] Ibid

[67] The Pioneer Newspaper, September 1897

[68] Ibid

[69] Lt-Col John Haughton, Commandant of the 36th Sikhs; A hero of Tirah, a memoir; A.C Yate, 1900, p118

[70] Historic records put his name ad Dad – but it is herein spelt Dadh to give better pronunciation of his name

[71] Their English counterparts carried the Lee-Metford which was a bolt action rifle introduced in 1894 but not given to native regiments for fear it would fall into enemy hands

[72] Old Steady Shots: The Martini-Henry Rifle, Rates of Fire and Effectiveness in the Anglo-Zulu War, Ian Knight

[73] Operations against the Orakzai Tribe on the Miranzai Frontiers under the command of Brigadier-General Sir W.S.A Lockhart in 1891, by Capt. A.H Mason, Simla, 1891, p58

[74] Ibid

[75] Ibid

[76] Ibid

[77] Ibid

[78] The Sheffield Grammar School magazine, February 1898

[79] Operations against the Orakzai Tribe on the Miranzai Frontiers under the command of Brigadier-General Sir W.S.A Lockhart in 1891, by Capt. A.H Mason, Simla, 1891, p59

[80] A lecture on how the Sikhs became a militant race / by M. Macauliffe, United Service Institution of India, [1903] (Simla : Government Central Printing Office)

[81] Authors interview with descendant Gurpreet Singh

[82] Operations against the Orakzai Tribe on the Miranzai Frontiers under the command of Brigadier-General Sir W.S.A Lockhart in 1891, by Capt. A.H Mason, Simla, 1891, p59

[83] Ibid

[84] Ibid

[85] Operations against the Orakzai Tribe on the Miranzai Frontiers under the command of Brigadier-General Sir W.S.A Lockhart in 1891, by Capt. A.H Mason, Simla, 1891, p60

[86] Letter written by J.A Lindsay from Fort Lockhart on 6th October 1897, from the collection of historian Byron Farwell
[87] Ibid p61
[88] Ibid, appendix J
[89] Ibid
[90] Ibid
[91] Lt-Col John Haughton, Commandant of the 36th Sikhs; A hero of Tirah, a memoir; A.C Yate, 1900, p142
[92] Presentation of Standards and Colours By His Royal Highness The Prince of Wales, 11 March 1922, Rawalpindi, p12
[93] Ibid
[94] Lt-Col John Haughton, Commandant of the 36th Sikhs; A hero of Tirah, a memoir; A.C Yate, 1900, p163
[95] Presentation of Standards and Colours By His Royal Highness The Prince of Wales, 11 March 1922, Rawalpindi, p13
[96] Operations against the Orakzai Tribe on the Miranzai Frontiers under the command of Brigadier-General Sir W.S.A Lockhart in 1891, by Capt. A.H Mason, Simla, 1891, p431
[97] Queen Victoria's Journals, volume 106, p60 www.queenvictoriasjournals.org
[98] Address to General Sir William Lockhart, Rawalpindi, 1898; from the archives of the National Army Museum
[99] The Nursing Record in 1897 via http://rcnarchive.rcn.org.uk/data/VOLUME019-1897/page354-volume19-30thoctober1897.pdf
[100] The Nursing Record in 1898, http://rcnarchive.rcn.org.uk/data/VOLUME021-1898/page197-volume21-3rdseptember1898.pdf
[101] Queen Victoria's Journals, volume 109, p62 www.queenvictoriasjournals.org
[102] Commander-in-Chief's speech at the Inauguration of the Sikh Memorial at Amritsar, from the original text
[103] Ibid
[104] Ibid
[105] Saragarhi Battalion: Ashes to Glory, History of the 4th Battalion the Sikh Regiment; Col. Kanwaljit Singh & Maj. H.S Ahluwalia, Lancer New Delhi, p23
[106] Ibid
[107] Sons of John Company: The Indian and Pakistan Armies 1903-1991; John Gaylor, Spellmount, p169
[108] Neil Carleton, Assistant Curator, Victoria and Albert Museum, London
[109] A lecture on how the Sikhs became a militant race / by M. Macauliffe, United Service Institution of India, [1903] (Simla : Government Central Printing Office)
[110] More information on this in the documentary "Sikhs At Sandhurst" available via www.sikhsatwar.info
[111] Bhagat Lakshman Singh, autobiography edited by Ganda Singh (1965)
[112] Ibid